IN THE SHADOW
OF THE FALCON

Chek shot vertically into the sky and began to climb, a thousand feet, two thousand, three, while below him the ravens followed, gaining height with remarkable speed. Seven thousand feet above the shimmering waters of the loch the ravens closed with him, and Chek found he could not get past their guard and escape in the sanctuary of a dive. Battered and buffeted by black wings, kicked and clawed, Chek was now in serious trouble. Desperately he twisted and turned, striking out at the heads of his opponents in an endeavour to stave off a lethal blow from their stabbing beaks.

Ewan Clarkson

IN THE SHADOW
OF THE FALCON

Illustrated by Victor Ambrus

ARROW BOOKS

ARROW BOOKS LTD
3 Fitzroy Square, London W1

An imprint of the Hutchinson Publishing Group

London Melbourne Sydney Auckland
Wellington Johannesburg Cape Town
and agencies throughout the world

First published in Great Britain by
Hutchinson & Co (*Publishers*) Ltd 1974
Arrow edition 1975
© Ewan Clarkson 1973
Illustrations © Hutchinson & Co
(*Publishers*) Ltd 1974

Made and printed in Great Britain
by The Anchor Press Ltd
Tiptree, Essex

ISBN 0 09 010800 3

To Jenkin Davies, friend of the falcons.

In The Shadow Of The Falcon

1

Return of the Wanderer

A shadow flickered fork-winged over the cliff. For a moment it hung poised, dark against the jade green surface of the sea. Then a small cloud drifted over the sun, and the shadow faded and was lost in a wilderness of crumbling, weatherworn rock and wind-rippled water.

Yet many eyes marked the passing of the shadow. It was seen by the buzzard as he swung in great wheeling circles, a thousand feet above the cliff. It was noticed by the raven as he perched motionless on a crag, high above his brooding mate. Even the tiny kestrel, hovering twenty feet above the newly plowed surface of a field, waiting for mice and beetles to show themselves, caught the flash of movement and life and filed the information away in his sharp little brain. The herring gulls shouted a warning, and the red billed chough screamed as he dived for the safety of the stones. Freya the wanderer, the peregrine falcon, had returned to her island stronghold.

A minute later and a mile away, a jackdaw died, its life blown out in an ash gray cloud of feathers that drifted away on the wind. Freya clutched her prize in the talons of her left foot and flapped away to a convenient platform of smooth rock, where she alighted and folded her wings. Still gripping her prey, she began to plume it, stripping the feathers away from the plump dark breast. When the flesh was naked she fed, cutting long strips of meat from the breastbone with her sharp curved beak and bolting them down with unhurried speed. From time to time she paused in her meal to gaze skyward or seaward with wild dark eyes, and always as she did so she crouched, as if ready for instant flight.

She was a large bird, some twenty inches in length from beak to tail and weighing just over thirty ounces. The feathers of her back and wings were the color of old, weatherworn slate—bluish gray—so that she was almost invisible against the cliff. Her chest and legs and the underparts of her wings were a deep cream, striated with marks of dark chestnut. Her talons and shanks were bright yellow, matching the cere of her bill. She wore a helmet of black, and her dark mustache and sideboards offset the white of her neck and throat. Her wings were long and pointed, and when at rest they reached two-thirds of the way down her tail.

Hunger satisfied, Freya wiped her bill with meticulous care, and leaving the corpse of the jackdaw to the buzzards and crows, she walked the few paces to the edge of the rock. She moved in an awkward, parrotlike fashion, almost hobbling, as though the rough stone was tender to her touch. Her talons, with their long, curving, razor-sharp claws, were instruments of death rather than locomotion, and, as always on land, she moved with extreme care, lest she should damage the needlelike points. Looking out to sea, she stretched her neck and gave voice, a high-pitched, staccato yelping. Then she sat back, her head half cocked, listening and waiting. The sun was westering, and sea and sky became one, in a soft diffusion of mist and golden light.

The answer came, faint but clear, from a speck in the sky high over the island. Lofting her wings, she launched herself from the rock and flew toward the newcomer, calling again as she climbed into the sky. The two birds met and circled, fell apart and climbed again, wheeling and spinning as the rays of the dying sun burnished their breasts with gold, so that they glittered like two stars high in the blue vault of the sky.

The land was warm from the March sun, and the air was rising, drawing a cold breeze off the sea. The peregrines rode the thermal and looked down on their territory, an island crouched in the Atlantic like a beast of prey, its shaggy head raised to the south, snarling defiance at the sea which had eaten away so much of the land.

The island was separated from the mainland by a narrow gut of water made turbulent with racing tides and armed with treacherous knife-edged rocks, half-hidden in the

13

foaming waves. Beyond, on the mainland, a broad promontory stretched eastward to the dark hills of Wales.

Except in the north, the mainland was flat, an intricate carpet of fields and bare pastures, a pattern of soft browns and muted greens, washed by the winter rains and bleached by the pale light of spring. A few small buildings lay scattered, like the discarded toys of some weary child, over the surface of the carpet, and the narrow roads were ribbons of white, flanked by the dark foliage of the gorse hedges.

To the north, a chain of shaggy hills reared five hundred feet above the waves. It was as if the gales of countless centuries had swept the land smooth, pushing to one side the great rocky mounds of resulting debris and leaving them to become clad with a rough growth of gorse and heather.

Three miles to the south lay the great bay of Saint Brides, its shore a shining scimitar of white sand, scoured by the surf that swept in from the Atlantic, and beyond that, lost in the hazy distance, another tongue of land probed out into the sea. To the west lay a scattering of islands, some mere rocks, weed-fringed and sea-washed, others, larger, thatched with a thick growth of grass, now withered and faded, bleached to the color of old bones.

In the gray of the spring twilight the two birds flew together to the west of the island, to pitch and roost on the high cliffs, merging and blending with the old gray rocks that towered above the Atlantic. The star Venus shone in the west, her brilliance eclipsing that of Jupiter, Antares, and old red Mars. All, save the sea, was still.

Morning dawned clear and cloudless. The sea was calm,

and a light frost spread a filigree of silver over the sleeping land. A solitary gull wailed, a sobbing cry that echoed and re-echoed among the caves and cliffs, rebounding from every rock and crevice.

The peregrines heard the call as they perched, motionless but alert, alone on their separate ledges. A hundred feet of cliff was all that lay between them, and a moment's flight would have united them, yet in spirit they were light years apart, for the ecstasy of union that had sent them spiraling together skyward had faded with the passing of the night. Now each was withdrawn, unaware of any need for the other. Yet the need was there, growing and stirring within them, swelling with the light, just as the bulbs of the wild hyacinths, hidden deep under the turf of the cliffs, were responding to the same call. As the earth tilted toward the sun, as the celandines bloomed and the gold of the gorse flung the glory of its wealth across the faded landscape, so their need would finally weld them in a union which nothing, save death, could sunder.

It was this need that had brought them back, to the little island of Ramsey and the cliff above the sea. Their lineage, and their claim to territory, was older than civilization, older than the Bronze Age men who had come with their herds and their womenfolk, seeking the gold and copper that lay hidden in the ground. Peregrines had nested on the cliff face before the sea came, when the cliff was an inland crag, towering high above forests and plains long since submerged beneath the waves.

High in the sky above the ancient plains, where bison and elk roamed, where the beaver worked his ancient craft,

15

carving his destiny and the shape of the land for centuries to come, a peregrine had killed. Primitive man, gripping his stone axe and gazing upwards with his uncanny, far-seeing stare, had seen the kill, had envied the bird and its skill in hunting. In that moment perhaps, an idea had been born, a concept that was to lead to a strange relationship between man and bird, a union of love and hate, a blend of slavery and freedom, the forging of a bond so finely wrought that it was invisible, yet so strong that a man could take a falcon on his fist and it would sit immobile, without fear, until it was allowed to fly free. Unleashed, the falcon would fly and kill, as free as the quarry it pursued, yet at the end it would return to the gloved fist.

Over the centuries men took and trained many species of falcons and hawks, from the noble peregrine to the dainty hobby and merlin, from the mighty goshawk to the diminutive sparrow hawk. Men scoured the earth in search of new varieties, taking gyrfalcon from the cold hills of Norway, lanner and saker from the dusty plains of Persia and Africa, and shaheen from the hot lands of India. There was more to their quest than mere pride of possession. It was as if, through his hawk, earthbound man found a new dimension of freedom, a chance to share the thrill of the flight, and the breathtaking stoop that preceded the kill.

The peregrine, of all the falcons, became the most treasured prize, the perquisite of royalty and nobility. Vast sums were paid to possess one, and the penalties for illegal ownership were swift and harsh.

The primacy of the peregrine may have been the result

of a voyage made by an English king across the sea from Wales to Ireland. As the ship passed Ramsey Island, the king stood on deck, bored and idle, surrounded by his courtiers, nursing his favorite goshawk and staring moodily out over the waves. A peregrine flew low over the rigging of the ship, and with a shout the king launched his goshawk. The great bird flew rapidly in pursuit, chopping the air with dark wings as it climbed above the falcon.

The engagement was brief. The peregrine sideslipped and fell, skimming the waves as the goshawk dropped, stiff-legged, talons outstretched to kill. The peregrine rose vertically and dived, a steel gray arrowhead that struck home, even as the gos turned to intercept. The dark form of the hawk crumpled and spiraled slowly down to the waves, where it drifted half-submerged, like the wreck of a once-proud galleon.

There was silence on board the ship, broken only by the slap of the sails and the creaking of timbers. Each of the courtiers waited anxiously, wondering how their lord would take this public humiliation. Their answer came in a mighty shout of royal laughter that shook his vast girth and brought relieved smiles to all present. From that day on the king would own no other bird save the descendants of the Pembrokeshire falcon that had slain a giant goshawk in fair combat.

Freya, the falcon, was a direct offspring of this line. Her mate Frika, the tiercel, now preening his nape on a nearby ledge, had drifted down from the far Northwest of Scotland. His grandparents had come from Norway, for the

17

peregrines were great wanderers and over the centuries had populated almost every country in the world. Most of them, after early wanderings, settled down to breed in the land of their birth, and so in time distinct races became established, but all wore the black helmet and the steel gray livery that was the badge of their lineage.

Now, without warning, the tiercel crouched and slipped off the ledge, diving almost to the surface of the sea before vanishing round the headland. The falcon watched him go and then began a slow and thorough examination of the cliff face. Time and the forces of erosion had wrought their slow handiwork on the rock, shaping and carving it wherever the stone was weakest. A great fissure ran vertically down the cliff face, terminating in the roof of a cave, and horizontal cracks formed wide ledges where sea pinks grew, and mosses and lichens clung.

A hundred and fifty feet above the cave the fissure widened to form the mouth of a narrow chamber, which tunneled far under the cliff. Above that was another, wider and shallower, and above that again was yet a third, just below the summit of the cliff. Each of these Freya visited in turn, waddling sedately around and peering upward, inspecting every detail of walls and roof and floor. Yet always, both on this first morning and on future visits, she returned to the first chamber, scratching the surface of the ledge and loosening the dry soil that lay hard packed on the rock.

Soon she had excavated a shallow, cuplike depression and had carried away several small stones, some pieces of rotten twig, and a few dried bones. A strange alchemy was at work in her blood, a driving force that she did not question or resist but obeyed as implicitly, as obediently, and as innocently as she followed the inner orders to kill.

2

The Dark Dancers

After the tiercel left the ledge he flew south for a while, his wing tips barely skimming the waves. Then, climbing, he passed over the island, and in a few moments he was crossing the Sound. The wind blew from the north, rippling the waves so that the waters of the Sound sparkled in the sun. The air was clear and cold, drying the bare brown soil of the fields, where already the farmers were busy planting potatoes.

Frika avoided the fields, with their bustle of activity and the noisy drone of tractor engines. Instead he flew south-east, over the cliffs, crossing heathland where the gorse bushes were dark against the yellow of the withered grass and the faded brown of the bracken. A young cock black-bird panicked at his approach, breaking cover from a gorse bush and swooping low over the rough, tussocky turf. Instantly, Frika darted in pursuit, his body suddenly tense with the instincts of the hunter.

The blackbird was too quick for him, the ground cover too dense. With a shrill scream of alarm, the young cock dived headlong into a seemingly impenetrable mass of bramble and briar thorn, where it crouched, hidden, chink-ing a warning to its kind. Chittering angrily, Frika flew on, still hugging the ground, skirting hedges and walls and lofting suddenly over outcrops of bare limestone rock, in the hope of surprising an unwary pigeon or jackdaw. At last he came to the marsh.

In summer the marsh was a mat of verdant green, fringed with the tall spears of yellow flag iris and bordered by leafy bushes of sallow. Now, after the rains of winter, it was a clear shallow pool of fresh water. A noisy chorus of gulls splashed and bickered in the morning sun, and a moor hen crept for cover, its head ducking nervously and its tail jerking as its broad-vaned toes propelled it through the water.

Frika ignored the gulls. They were hard to catch, and their stringy, rancid flesh a poor reward for so much effort. Avoiding the open water, he skirted the margins, darting from side to side in an endeavor to flush some unwary bird into flight.

At the top of the pool he was rewarded. A lonely green sandpiper, probing the mud for insects, was startled into flight. He climbed high and piped as he flew, his white rump flashing in the sun. Frika launched himself in pursuit, and though the sandpiper was fast, the tiercel soon gained on him, climbing above him with short, chopping wing beats. The sandpiper turned and swung in a wide arc, dropping in a last desperate attempt to gain the safety of the marsh, but Frika had closed his wings and was diving for the kill. His talons were bunched tight against his chest, and the wind whistled past him. The earth lurched dizzily up toward him and the sandpiper's back grew broad and large in his vision.

As he swept past his victim, Frika's talons shot out, striking the sandpiper at the base of his neck. An explosion of feathers filled the sky, and a spatter of crimson fell to the lake, as Frika caught the lifeless body of the sandpiper in mid-air and flew triumphantly away.

Fifteen minutes later little was left of the sandpiper save the intestines, which Frika had drawn fastidiously aside, and the high bare keel of the breastbone, picked clean and deeply notched by the tiercel's sharp curved beak. The pinions, still attached to the skeleton by bare bones, stirred slightly in the wind as Frika picked up the green shank of the sandpiper in his beak and threw it back into his now-distended crop. In spite of repeated gulpings one foot remained obstinately outside his beak, and after a few moments Frika shook his head and threw the leg away. He wiped his beak, stretched luxuriously, first the right leg and wing, then the left, shook himself until all his feathers were ruffled, and then dozed a while, as the sun warmed his back and the wind riffled the fine feathers of his flanks.

The deep croak of a raven passing overhead woke him to

instant alertness. Immediately he remembered the cliff face, and Freya, the falcon. Spreading his wings, he flung himself off the rock, climbed high, and with rapid wing beats flew purposefully toward the island, dodging a half-hearted lunge from the raven, whose mate was brooding a clutch of green and brown speckled eggs on the cliff below. The raven followed him at a discreet distance. He had no great desire to join combat with the peregrine but was anxious to see him safely off his territory. As soon as he had escorted Frika out over the waters of the Sound he returned to his mate on her nest of heather twigs.

Freya was still pottering among the crevices on the cliff face and barely noticed Frika's return. Less than an hour had passed since his departure, and the day was still young. Frika pitched on a ledge, away from the wind and warmed by the morning sun, and sat impassive, motionless, survey-ing the surrounding seascape.

The sea was largely empty. Plankton had just begun to bloom, to grow and swell into the rich sea pastures that would support a vast wealth of marine life, which in turn would feed the sea birds soon to arrive. On the land, as in the sea, growth was hidden, stirring beneath the soil, yet still sheltering from the last dying but dangerous bite of winter. On the cliffs, a few flowers braved the cold—shy purple violets and golden star sprays of celandines, hugging the ground and shielded by the dead dry stems of withered grass and fern.

At the foot of the cliffs a small colony of herring gulls squabbled over nesting sites. The air was loud with their clamor, and from time to time a fight broke out, the contestants buffeting each other with their wings and using their beaks to drag each other off the ledges. Soon all would be order and peace, as one by one each individual claimed victory, or accepted defeat.

For most of the residents, those who had remained to face the rigors of winter rather than risk the lottery of migration, it was a time for relaxation, a chance to laze in the sun before shouldering the responsibilities of raising a family. The cormorant perched upright on a rock, his wings outstretched to the sun, looking like some ancient symbol of heraldry, and a bull seal rolled lazily, before sinking back into the clear green water.

A shrill scream split the air, dying abruptly, like the ricochet of a spent bullet. From a low ledge of stone that jutted out into the Atlantic one black shape emerged, was joined by another, and yet another, until there were eight of them, rising and falling, dancing in the bright spring air. The birds were choughs, sable-plumaged, with bright red beaks and legs, so delicately built that they resembled big black butterflies. They seemed to float rather than fly, as they danced their aerial ballet.

Now the flock split into two groups of four, and their cries grew more excited as they climbed into the air. The quartets divided again, each pair flying in close unison, black blossoms blown on the wind of courtship. Then it was over, and the flock settled sedately on the rock.

For a brief while the dark dancers would soak in the spring sunlight, and then one by one each pair would steal away, to vanish among the tumbled masses of slate and crumbling, weatherworn granite, seeking some deep dark crevice in which to build their nests and raise their young. Fate had dealt harshly with this, the most graceful of the crow family. Once their screams had echoed around the high cliffs from Sussex to Land's End and throughout the Cornish coast, but now their numbers had dwindled until only a few survivors remained, sheltering in the remote cliffs of Wales, Ireland, and Northwest Scotland.

The day wore on. The sun reached the zenith of its short climb, passed to the south of the island, and began to sink into the Atlantic. Freya began to feel the pangs of hunger and slipped off the ledge where for the past hour she had sat preening, coaxing and worrying each disheveled feather until it sat tight and clean in its correct place. Frika joined her, and together they climbed over the island to circle above the Sound.

At first the thrill of flight, and the joy of being alive in the company of her mate, made Freya forget her hunger, to wheel and soar in the clear evening sky. Throughout the centuries the peregrines had flown thus, their breasts burnished by the evening light. The warriors of old, watching, had at once seen their resemblance to enchanted axe heads, sickle-shaped, lethal, forged by the fire of the sun and gifted with the power of flight. So they came to be called falcons, the twin curving crescents of their wings distinguishing them from the round-winged hawks.

Equally obvious, as they soared together, was the difference in size between Freya and her mate. He was fully three inches shorter, smaller boned, and less powerful, weighing no more than twenty ounces. So he earned his title of tiercel, being a third smaller in size than the falcon.

The light was fading. The peregrines sensed this and ceased their soaring, riding the wind currents and hanging motionless in the sky, alert, watchful, suddenly impelled by the urgent need to hunt and kill. This was the hour when weary birds were winging their way to roost, their crops full, their senses a little less alert.

Three pigeons flew down the Sound, making for their roosting place on the cliff. Frika closed his wings and dropped, passing between their ranks and scattering them in all directions as he broke his dive and climbed rapidly among them. Two of the pigeons flew for the cliffs, but the third turned out over the Sound, ascending with frantic wing beats as Frika darted in pursuit.

Freya waited five hundred feet above the waves. She marked the fleeing path of the pigeon, with Frika's dark form snaking in the rear, and came in a long shallow dive, accelerating every second. At the last moment the pigeon twisted aside, and Freya's talons kicked empty air as she sped on, to turn and come chopping back. As she climbed above her quarry, Frika, in a sudden explosive burst of energy, passed underneath the pigeon and turning on his back, plucked the bird out of the skies. Frika's talons closed, the pigeon flapped madly for a second, and then hung limp, its life crushed out.

Frika bore his prize skyward as Freya, shouting her anger and frustration, climbed in hot pursuit. When she was but a few feet below him he released his grip on the bird, and Freya caught it as it spiraled downward. Frika followed her to the cliff and landed on the ledge close to his mate. Freya was already at work, tearing avidly at the hot flesh, guarding her prey with mantled, hooded wings, and hissing jealously whenever Frika showed the slightest interest. Frika was unconcerned. As the last light left the sea and the land grew dark, his eyelids drooped, then closed. His head sank into his breast, and he slept.

3

Island Stronghold

April came, and as the days lengthened, the sun warmed the land. The gorse flowers flamed in the hedgerows, ringing the fields with cloth of gold, while on the cliffs pale primroses spread like constellations of wan stars amid the butter-yellow blossoms of the cowslips. Each species had its own time and season, yet always a few adventurers emerged early, to mingle with the last survivors of an earlier flower. Every dip and fold in the cliff held its own micro climate, encouraging early growth here, retarding it elsewhere. So it was possible to find early hyacinths spread in a thin purple veil, while still a few late snowdrops lingered nearby.

Each evening, as the sun set, staining the sky and silver-

ing the steel gray of the sea, the peregrines flew their courtship flight, sometimes climbing so high that when the earth
lay in the darkness of its own shadow their breasts were
still burnished by the sun's rays. Each evening Frika grew
more ardent in his courtship, and Freya accepted and
invited his caresses, prostrating herself with drooping wings
and widespread tail, crooning softly all the while.

One morning, in the soft light of early dawn, as the sea
lay oily and calm, bound by swathes of thick gray mist,
Freya slipped quietly into the niche she had chosen as her
eyrie. For a long time she remained hidden, and only the
deep triple boom of the foghorn from the lighthouse to the
west broke the silence. When she emerged, the fog had
begun to disperse, pale blue sky shone among the shreds of
cloud, and on the soft brown earth of the hollow in the
niche lay an egg.

The next morning there was another, and on the following day yet a third, slightly smaller than the others. The
eggs were large and round, sharply pointed at one end, the
shells so heavily blotched with russet markings that the
deep cream of the background was barely discernible.
They lay without touching in the dim light of the eyrie.

Frika was intrigued. Freya allowed him to inspect the
clutch from the ledge outside the eyrie, but when he
attempted to enter she drove him off with such asperity
that he flew yelping to the furthermost ledge on the cliff
face. There he sat, shaking his feathers and moodily
scratching at the lice that infested his head and neck.

Gingerly, Freya stalked into the eyrie and settled on her
eggs, fluffing her feathers and letting her wings hang
loosely at her sides. On her breast were patches of skin

where the feathers did not grow, and these areas—the brood patches—were swollen and engorged with blood, so that they were hotter than the rest of her body. It was comforting to feel the cool hard surface of the eggs pressed smooth against these areas, and she fell into a doze.

Frika went hunting, to return after a short while with the warm limp body of a thrush, its beak still stained with the mud it had been gathering to line its nest. Frika carried the thrush to a ledge, where he carefully plumed it before flapping over to the eyrie. Freya opened her eyes and gave a soft hunger cry but made no attempt to move, so Frika fed her, cutting thin slivers of flesh from the plump breast of the thrush. Freya took each piece as he offered it to her, sometimes gently, almost tenderly; sometimes, when he was slower than usual in preparing the morsel, snatching it from his beak with a violence and greed that made him blink.

When most of the breast had gone she turned her head away, her eyelids drooping once more in sleep. Frika flew to a nearby ledge and ate the head and legs of the thrush. The high, keeled breastbone, with the wings still attached, he left on the ledge, where a moment later a gust of wind caught it. The remains, light and buoyant, stirred as if in resurrection, drifted off the ledge, and began their last slow spiraling flight down to the waves. A patrolling herring gull marked their flight and, wheeling, he swooped down to alight on the sea beside them. In a moment he was joined by other gulls, and between them they tore the carcass apart, wolfing down bone and feather with throaty cries of greed and satisfaction. Nothing was wasted.

The day wore on, and the rays of the westering sun inched their slow pathway over the cliff face. The old gray rocks soaked up the light and shone with a dim luster, revealing hidden hues of soft purple and sage green, dusky pink and mauve, each crack and crevice bold-etched in violet shadow. At last the sun pitched warm and yellow on the entrance to the eyrie, waking Freya with its caress.

Easing herself off her eggs, Freya walked on to the ledge in front of the eyrie and stood blinking in the strong light. Slowly, she stretched, first one leg and wing, then the other. Then she shook her feathers so that they ruffled all around her before easing back into place. Gazing about her she called, an urgent, high pitched summons, and Frika answering, flew off his ledge. Together they lofted high in the sky above the cliffs, hanging motionless, riding the wind that blew in a steady stream from the sea. The eggs lay almost invisible on the soil of the eyrie, cooling a little but guarded against a sudden chill by the warmth of the sun.

The eyrie Freya had chosen had many qualities that made it superior to other nesting sites on the cliff. It was virtually inaccessible to other than winged predators, for the cliff below rose vertically from the sea, while, above, it was protected by an overhang of rock. It commanded a wide view, which gave early warning of a passing pigeon or the approach of an enemy. It was dry and well drained and sheltered from the worst of the winds, for although it faced north of west, a neighboring arm of cliff swept round and out to sea, forming a small bay, and breaking the strength of the worst gales.

Except in the late afternoon the eyrie lay in shadow. This again was important, ensuring Freya's comfort, a well as giving her a chance to leave her eggs for the brief while that the sun lay upon them. Later on, when the summer sun beat down on the land and cast its fierce glare on the sea, the young peregrines would be spared from its heat, yet be guaranteed a gentle warmth before the night, with, perhaps, a chance to dry plumage that had been soaked by a summer shower.

For these reasons the eyrie had been chosen, not only by Freya, but by countless generations of peregrines. Each spring, century after century, the falcons had returned to their ancestral homes. Each occupant was imbued with a strong sense of territory, and the pair guarded their domain with jealous pride, refusing to tolerate any intruding peregrines within a radius of four or five miles.

One flaw marred the perfection of this arrangement. Man had a memory. Man had ropes and climbing gear, and man had motive. The very permanence of the eyries proved their weakness, for once a man had established the whereabouts of a nesting site, he could return year after year to take the eggs and young.

In medieval times serfs risked life and limb to take the young falcons for the benefit of royalty and nobility, but their depredations were few and the very isolation of the eyries was protection enough. Then came the invention of the breech-loading shotgun, and with it the concept of raising huge heads of game for the winter entertainment of shooting parties. Any natural predators which presumed to take what man considered his rightful property were ruthlessly destroyed, and keepers were employed for this duty.

So from his proud perch on the fist of a nobleman, the

peregrine fell to an ignoble end, hanging head-down on a keeper's gibbet, in company with the rotting corpses of buzzards, crows and owls, stoats, weasels, and polecats.

At the same time the spread of the railways opened up whole new territories for the adventurous Victorians and Edwardians to explore. With their insatiable appetite for collecting, and their interest in the pseudo-scientific hobby of natural history, they plundered the eyries for their eggs, frequently taking the entire clutch. Young birds too were taken, for although the art of falconry had declined, there were still many men prepared to pay a handsome price for a bird that was once the proudest possession of a king.

Still the peregrines survived as a breed, although in such declining numbers that some men, more farseeing than others, grew concerned for their future. Eventually the peregrine and its eggs became protected by law, but in spite of this, illicit egg-collecting still went on, and even on her remote island, Freya was not entirely safe.

Freya was ignorant of the history of her race, but she knew well the dangers of leaving her eggs unguarded for too long. Even in the eyrie they could be discovered by some marauding raven or black-backed gull, and as the minutes passed she grew increasingly anxious. At last, dropping out of the sky, she swooped down almost to sea level, before sweeping up the face of the cliff to land on the ledge. All was well, the eggs were still as she had left them, and crooning softly to herself, Freya settled down once more.

Frika watched her disappear into the eyrie and then flew off, passing south of the island, and crossing the Sound to the mainland. In a shallow valley leading down to a small cove an oak tree grew, halfway up a low cliff of crumbling rock. The oak tree had been planted by a peregrine. Over a century ago, at dusk on a gusty October evening, a wood pigeon had hacked its way over the valley, its crop laden with acorns. A peregrine, poised in the air above the cliffs, had marked the flight of the bird and had come in on a long, shallow dive, hitting the pigeon squarely on the back of the neck.

The force of the blow had burst open the pigeon's crop, spilling the acorns so that they bounced and scattered in a hard rain over the valley. Some were damaged by the fall, and others were later found and eaten by rabbits and sheep. One had survived, lodged deep in a crack in the rock, where the rotting debris of centuries provided a soft bed. The oak had grown until it had reached the top of the cliff, and then the crown had flattened out, the foliage eternally cropped by the searing salt wind that blew over the headland. So the tree had survived, never prospering, but never quite relinquishing its hold on life, and each year a crow had nested in its branches.

Frika lighted on the oak, close by the massive black bulk of the nest. Barely had he settled before the parent birds were all around him, the air filled with their angry cries, their dusty black wings beating and buffeting him, their beaks and scaly legs striking out at his face and head. Frika fled, climbing vertically into the sky before leveling out and making for the sea. The cock crow soon abandoned the chase, but the hen crow continued to pursue him, gaining on him with strong wing beats, and harrying him from the rear. In exasperation, Frika fell back and below her. Then climbing, he stooped and kicked out as he passed.

It seemed that he had missed his mark, but the crow fell in a tumbling dive, only regaining her level flight a few feet above the land. Shaking her head and cawing dismally, she flew back to the oak, where she sat, hunched and shivering, one eye tightly closed. One claw of Frika's had found its mark, piercing her right eyeball, and though the wound healed, the sight in that eye grew misty and blurred. As the days passed it faded altogether, and the eye became a dead, chalky white.

Frika flew on, skirting the cliffs and dropping down into the rocky cove at the foot of the valley. Whimbrel were coming in on the tide, dropping down onto the weed-covered rocks that lined the shore and pausing in low, murmured conversation before stepping cautiously into the swirling foam to probe for small shellfish and crabs or to dig in the sand for worms. They were on their way north, to their breeding grounds in the Arctic circle, after a winter by the hot shores of Africa.

Most of the flock froze, crouching tight to the brown weed, as Frika swept among them, but a small knot of birds rose from the wet sand with twittering cries of fear, scattering out over the sea and away from the safety and shelter of the rocks. Singling out one bird, Frika dove beneath it, forcing it up and away from the water and into the open sky. He killed it skillfully, almost languidly, before beginning the long slow flight back to the eyrie with his burden.

Freya scolded him for his long absence, before attacking the corpse of the whimbrel, gorging herself on the flesh until little remained for the tiercel. Frika carried the remains over to his favorite ledge and picked them over for a

few moments before dropping them in the sea. The light was fading, but there was still time for a quick kill. Passing over the cliffs, he skimmed the thick heather that bordered the hill. The island was overrun with rabbits, and the young were just beginning to emerge, to crop the grass in the soft light of evening. Frika dropped on one as it strayed from the shelter of a gorse bush, and its dying squeal was muffled by the beating of his wings.

4

The Doves of War

To the casual observer, the rocky ramparts of the cliffs seemed grim and forbidding, an environment so harsh as to make the struggle for survival an unending and relentless task. Yet this was not the case. For the peregrines and the sea birds, and the sleek gray seals that lay on the rocks below, the cliffs were at once a sanctuary and a fortress.

For the sea birds, the warm womb of the ocean poured forth an endless supply of food that was rich, nourishing, and easy to obtain. Above all, the white light of the sun, the clean cold winds that swept in from the sea, and the stinging showers of rain, preserved an atmosphere of antiseptic purity, without which such densely packed communities would swiftly perish from disease. So the auks and the gulls and the kittiwakes not only survived but enjoyed a health and vigor such as most men had forgotten, their communities a strong contrast with the squalid cities of man.

Other creatures shared the life of the sea cliffs. Nearly all the members of the crow family were there—the jackdaw, the raven, the crow, and the chough. Only the rook preferred to nest in the high tops of the deanery elms, and to till the fallow fields with his great plowshare of a beak.

From the dark depths of a sea cave came the soft cooing of a dove. Inside the cave, on ledges just below the roof, were five untidy nests, loosely woven from heather stems and dried seaweed, each containing two white eggs. In the semi-darkness, the parent birds brooded their eggs or perched close by on the ledges, crooning in the quiet contentment of each other's company. Their history and the story of their association with mankind was as old, if not older, than the story of the peregrine, and in many ways stranger.

Of the five pairs of birds in the cave, no two were exactly alike. Some wore a plumage of cinnamon and white, some were piebald. Others were varying shades of dove gray, but only two wore the true livery of the rock dove—the white rump, the black wing bars, and the iridescent neck patch of green and purple. Even these two were not descended from pure wild stock, for the true rock dove had long been extinct on these cliffs and every bird had either been born in captivity or was the descendant of domesticated stock.

When man the hunter became man the farmer, he was

quick to notice that these fat gray birds, which were so delicious to eat, came readily to his settlements to feed on spilled grain and scraps that lay around. So he began to capture and domesticate the rock dove, and long before travelers to the Far East returned with chickens, the domesticated offspring of the jungle fowl which laid such a plentiful supply of large eggs, the dove was a familiar sight in ancient cities.

Soon man discovered another useful trait that the dove possessed. The bird had a strongly developed territorial instinct and so could be kept in a loft or cote, flying free each day and returning each evening after foraging far afield. So the owners discovered how to obtain a plentiful supply of meat at little expense to themselves, meat which would help to nourish man through the winter, when other food was scarce.

It soon occurred to man that this homing instinct could be put to further use, for even when transported long distances from its home the pigeon would return, flying at speeds of up to sixty miles an hour and traveling hundreds of miles without stopping. So when travelers set off on a long journey, or armies went to war, pigeons were carried, and when released with a written message strapped to their leg, would fly swiftly and surely home, bearing news of safe arrival, victory or defeat, or summoning help if need be. In time much of the world's commerce and trade came to depend on the services of the carrier pigeon.

So the centuries passed, and man began to breed new varieties of pigeon from the native rock doves. Some were brought back to Britain after the Crusades, and as they had done with the peregrine, nobility reserved the right to keep pigeons for themselves and inflicted severe penalties on any peasant who tried to do the same.

Inevitably, some birds escaped from captivity and instead of returning to their home loft, settled down in their natural homes on the cliffs. Several of the birds in the cave were descended from ancestors once reared in the dovecotes of the monastery at Saint David's, on the mainland. More escaped as gradually the food value of the pigeon declined and the practice of keeping them was allowed to spread among what were considered to be the lower classes.

In the latter half of the nineteenth century the workers of an industrial nation turned to the breeding of pigeons as a cheap and absorbing hobby. Particularly exciting was the practice of racing pigeons. The pastime grew, attracting hundreds of thousands of devotees, and spreading across the Western world. Considerable sums of money were at stake, and a good homer could be worth hundreds of pounds to its owner.

As the twentieth century ground on and the great nations of the world turned toward competition of a grimmer, sterner kind, pigeon fanciers noticed that frequently homers failed to return from a race, even when weather conditions were favorable. The answer to the disappearance of the racing birds was to be found in many a peregrine eyrie, buried among the debris on the ledge, for there among the anonymous bones and wing feathers lay numbers of aluminum rings, each bearing the legend N.U.R.P., the initials of the National Union of Racing Pigeons.

So war was declared on the peregrine once more, and in

addition to the attacks from gamekeepers and egg collectors, the peregrine had to face the explosive wrath of the pigeon fanciers. Birds died, shot without compunction. Their eyries were violated, the eggs smashed, and young birds killed.

Fortunately for the peregrine, a strong body of sympathizers felt that the extinction of the peregrine was too high a price to pay for the benefit of a minority of pigeon fanciers, and as a result of their agitation, the peregrine became protected by law. Their relief was to be short lived.

As the shadow of the swastika fell across Europe, deepening and darkening until it threatened to blot the light of truth from the world, the peregrine was declared an ally of the Axis powers. The British fighting forces still relied on carrier pigeons to convey messages in time of war. In particular, airplanes spotting submarines off the coasts had to maintain radio silence, lest their quarry should learn that they had been detected. They used pigeons to carry information of the submarines' whereabouts, and a pigeon flying in to the coast from the sea was a prime target for a peregrine.

So the Air Ministry decided that in order to safeguard the national interest, all peregrines should be destroyed. In order that peregrines only should be destroyed, and not other birds of prey, experienced naturalists all over the country were contacted and asked to give their aid in this task. All agreed, although not without deep regret at having to perform such a disagreeable duty. To assist them in their work, they were given financial aid and a gasoline ration, and in order to make the execution of the peregrine a legal act, its name was struck from the list of protected birds.

In spite of all precautions, other, harmless birds of prey were killed. Following the news that the peregrine was to be exterminated around the coasts, the keeper of a lighthouse noticed a pair of falcons hanging around the cliffs. He took his gun and shot one of the pair, which fell into the sea and was lost. On the evening of the second day he shot the other bird, and this time he was able to retrieve the corpse. He sent it to a naturalist on the mainland, with a letter of explanation. The naturalist read the letter and then opened the accompanying parcel. Inside lay the bloodstained corpse of a kestrel.

So thoroughly and ruthlessly were the peregrines persecuted that in many areas, particularly in the south, where peregrine eyries had existed for centuries, the annihilation of the falcons was complete. Over six hundred birds, old and young, were killed and countless eggs destroyed. Breeding birds, which for one reason or another could not be shot, were provided with dummy eggs made of plaster of paris, and the falcons brooded these, instead of laying a second clutch.

Even before the end of the war there were signs that the destruction of the peregrines was not altogether a good thing. The wild descendants of the captive pigeons, free from harassment by their ancestral enemy, multiplied at an unprecedented rate. Colonies from the cliffs raided coastal farms and plundered valuable foodstuffs, while in the towns and cities pigeons fouled buildings and pavements and blocked gutters with their untidy nests. Inland, flocks of wood pigeons stripped the fields of grain and greenstuff to such a degree that pigeon shoots were hurriedly organized to combat the menace.

About this time someone remembered that during the Crusades, King Richard had organized a company of falconers to disrupt the carrier-pigeon service of the Turks and this had proved so successful that it was thought possible that a similar falcon unit might be effective against Axis carrier pigeons. The Air Ministry also became interested in the idea of training falcons. Birds of all descriptions had been flocking to the airports, and in the resulting collisions between aircraft and birds, many planes were damaged, and some had actually crashed. It was thought that the presence of falcons on and around the airports might prove a deterrent to other birds. So a fresh search began, and the countryside scoured for eyas peregrines suitable for training.

By the end of the war, when the peregrine was once more restored to the protected list, it was feared that the falcons had become so rare that they would never recover as a breeding species. Yet during the war years many remote areas of moor and mountain, which before the war had been strictly preserved for game shooting, had been neglected. The gamekeepers had been called to service with the armed forces, or they had found work of more vital importance. So it was here that the peregrines lasted out the war, and from these strongholds they came back, to recolonize the empty eyries and to prosper on the abundant stocks of pigeons. Within ten years they had almost regained their previous numbers, and though still rare, it seemed they would survive as a breed.

Not all the carrier and racing pigeons which failed to return to their lofts fell victim to the peregrines, or to any other predator. Many simply deserted and returned to the wild. Among the colony of pigeons in the cave was a racing homer. Three times this pigeon had raced, and each time it had won. Its owner was young and inexperienced, too eager, when the pigeon arrived in its home loft, to catch the bird and remove from its leg the red rubber race-band. This band, when inserted in a special time clock, would record the flight time, and so every second's delay in obtaining the record prejudiced the bird's chances of winning. Consequently, each time the bird had returned home it had been roughly handled and frightened.

On its next flight, instead of associating thoughts of its home loft with the pleasures of food and warmth and comfort, the pigeon remembered only the fear and discomfort it had suffered, and so flew reluctantly, obeying the call of instinct without enthusiasm. Sighting a flock of wild doves feeding in a stubble field, it dropped down among them, and when night came it flew with them to roost on the cliffs. Now, although it still wore the indestructible aluminum ring, the rubber race ring had long since perished, and with it all recollection of the North Country loft in which the bird had been born. For two seasons now it had bred in the cave, giving with the blood of its line strength and swiftness to its offspring. Freya knew the pigeon well, and knew that unless she could catch it unawares, it would have to be a hard, swift stoop indeed to give her power enough to overtake and stop the bird in flight.

So Freya ignored the pigeon. Always there was other,

easier prey, smaller or slower on the wing. Had Freya been imbued with human motives and desires, she might have regarded the pigeon as a challenge and a test of her skill as a huntress. But Freya was a falcon, and there was no place in falcon philosophy for ambition or the continual need to strive toward success. To survive was sufficient in itself.

5

The Guardian

The island was large enough to support a small farm, and tucked away in a sheltered cove to the northeast of the island stood the house, a long, low-roofed building of whitewashed stone, which looked out toward the mainland and the shaggy, towering head of Carn Llidi. The cove provided a natural harbor, the only safe landfall when the winds blew and the sea leaped in anger against the precipitous cliffs on the western side of the island. Even here landing was not always safe, and never easy, for the savage tides that ripped through the sound, laying bare the sharp-fanged rocks of the Bitches, together with the heaving swell of the ground sea, made maneuvering a boat a tricky procedure.

At the farm lived a man, a widower. When the war in Europe had ended, Owen Thomas had left the sea, and the ships that had been his livelihood since he was a child, and had settled on the island. He lived alone, for both his daughters had married and gone away, while his son had followed him in his profession as a sailor and was now an engineer on an oil tanker.

He was alone but not lonely, for he loved the solitude and the eternal, ever-changing song of the sea. He had a deep and abiding interest in the island and the wealth of wild life that it supported, and over the years his name and his experience as a naturalist had made him many friends.

On the rich soil of the tiny fields that lay scattered over the northern half of the island he grew hay and some corn. He raised beef cattle and sheep, which grazed over the clifftops and the moorland to the south, and he kept chickens and ducks. The farm brought him little profit, but he was self-supporting and his needs were few. His one luxury in life was a glass of whiskey, in the evenings when his work was done, and much of this was supplied by visiting bird watchers, who well knew his fondness for the golden liquid.

He was equally at home on the sea, rowing among the rocks at low tide to set lobster pots or drifting with the tide and spinning for mackerel on a summer's evening. Regularly he rowed across the Sound to the mainland and walked a mile and a half to the tiny cathedral city of Saint David's for his few provisions. Although he had now reached the age when most men were beginning to think of retiring, he was fit and hale, short in stature, thick-set rather than fat, with great strength in his arms and legs. His thick dark hair was just beginning to show the first frosting of white, and his sight was as keen as a hawk's.

He knew about the presence of the peregrines on the eyrie and had noted the date of their arrival in his field diary. Each evening he watched them, lying spread-eagled on the short turf of the headland opposite the nesting site and peering through his old brass telescope until his eyes watered with the strain and his fingers were numb with cold from the chill winds of spring. He chuckled to himself at the occasional bickering of the pair, and in his imagination he soared with them on their evening flights over the sea.

All the same, he was anxious. He knew of the rarity of the falcons, and he knew also that there were still individuals callous and greedy enough to wish to take the eggs or young. The rougher element among the laborers on the mainland would not hesitate if they knew that there was money to be made from such vandalism, and soon they would be joined by itinerant workers, potato pickers from all parts of Wales and Ireland.

Up to a point, he could protect the peregrines. The only safe landing was in view of his home, and he could send anyone packing whom he did not entirely trust. Yet he knew that in fine weather a yacht could anchor off the beach known as Aber Mawr, and from there a small boat could row ashore. Then a short scramble up the cliffs would put an intruder right above the eyrie. They would need ropes and stakes, and an hour or two in which to work, but he could not always be on guard. At dawn, or when he was at work in the fields, or over on the mainland, there would be plenty of time. During the day he found his mind returning again and again to the problem, and at night he lay awake, wondering how best to protect what he had come to regard as his birds and praying for a solution.

He found the answer in a yellowhammer's nest. One morning, as he drove the house cow out beyond the fields to graze on the fresh new grass that was springing up on the clifftops, he found the delicately woven cup of plaited grass on the ground beside a low stone wall. Carefully, he marked the spot, so that he would not accidentally disturb the nest on some future occasion. Then he stood for a moment in the sunshine, admiring the soft, pale pink luster of the eggs and the curious markings that looked as though someone had taken a pen and scribbled all over them. Suddenly he knew that he had found a way to safeguard the eggs of the peregrine. He would have to wait for evening, when the falcon was off the eyrie, but all day, as he went about his tasks, his mind was busy with his plan.

After supper he set off to the cliffs, a bundle slung over his shoulder. It was a weighty burden—two stout iron stakes, a sledgehammer, a long coil of thick rope, a shorter length of thinner cord, a sack, and four wooden stakes. He was hot and panting by the time he reached the cliff above the eyrie, but he did not rest for long. Dropping his load on the turf, he took the four wooden stakes and walked around to the headland opposite the eyrie.

As he had hoped, the peregrines were flighting. Freya, a mile to the north and a thousand feet above the waves, had seen him toiling up the hill, but he was a familiar figure to the peregrines and they had long since accepted him as harmless. Freya slanted away on the wind and vanished behind the cliffs.

Because of the overhang, he could not tell from above exactly where the eyrie lay, and had he tried to guess, he might have found himself hanging in mid-air, several feet to the right or left of the spot. Now he was about to set markers which would give him the exact location of the site.

He pushed one of the stakes into the soft turf, and walking backwards about twenty paces, he stuck a second one into the ground, carefully positioning it so that the two stakes were exactly in line with the eyrie. Then he walked fifty paces to the right, and did the same with the other two stakes. Now returning to the cliff above the eyrie, he looked back across the bay. He could see that the point where he had dropped his bundle was a little too far to the left. Moving it, he stood at last at a point from which, as he looked across the bay, the two farthermost stakes were directly in line, and therefore hidden, by the ones in front. This point was right above the eyrie.

Swiftly he drove the stakes that were to hold the rope into the ground, one behind the other, and lashed them together with the thin cord. Even if one began to loosen, the other would hold. Then he anchored the rope, knotting it securely to the stake below the lashing. He slung the free end of the rope down over the cliff, slipped the sack under it to prevent the rough rock from fraying the hempen fibers and, without hesitating, began to lower himself hand over hand, down the cliff.

At first the going was easy, but as he reached the over-

54

hang the rope began to bind against the rock, crushing his knuckles against the rough stone and tearing his skin. His booted feet lost their grip on the cliff face, and he twined his ankles around the rope. He wished he had thought of wearing canvas shoes and gloves, but it was too late to turn back now. Many times in the past he had climbed down the cliffs, mainly to take the eggs of the murderous black-backed gulls, which in recent years had grown too numerous for the good of other sea birds, but the gulls had nested on gentler, less precipitous slopes. Now he wondered if perhaps he was not growing too old for cliff climbing. Already his arms were beginning to feel the strain.

At last he passed the overhang and made rapid progress down to the ledge. He had imagined the distance to be about twenty feet, but as he counted each slow handhold, he realized that he had considerably underestimated the drop. The wind seemed to sweep up the cliff face, buffeting him and making him sway on the rope. Loose particles of shale rained down on him, and his arms began to ache.

After thirty handholds he risked a quick glance down, and the sudden wave of nausea and vertigo that assailed him as he glimpsed the white waves heaving and tossing at the base of the cliff made his heart lurch. The ledge was only a few feet below him now, and he lowered himself another handhold. Then the rope began to twist, spinning him slowly around and around.

For a moment he panicked, and almost fell. Then, with eyes tight shut, he thrust his feet out at right angles to the rope, and felt the spinning stop as his boots thudded against the rock. Next moment he was on the ledge, and he rested, taking deep shuddering breaths as he strove to quiet his thudding heart. Then, still keeping hold of the rope, he knelt and peered into the eyrie.

He knew then, for a brief instant, something of the motives and desires that drove men to plunder the nests of rare birds. The eggs looked so beautiful, so solid and rich and rare as they lay on the bare soil, that it was like gazing on hidden treasure. The feeling was intensified as, tucking the rope securely under one knee, he reached forward and picked up the first egg. It even felt valuable, as if made of gold, and he felt a curious reluctance to put it down.

He pulled himself together. There was no time to waste, for at any moment the peregrines might return. There was little danger. The birds were unlikely to attack him, but he knew that their rage and fear over his presence at the eyrie might cause them to desert their precious eggs. Fumbling in his pocket, he produced an indelible pencil. Using his forefinger, he moistened the egg with saliva, and then, as thickly and firmly as he dared, he printed the word: INDELIBLE. Each egg was thus marked, and so ruined as a collector's item, for the writing could not be erased without also destroying the magnificent mottling that identified the eggs as those of the peregrine falcon.

Carefully he arranged the eggs exactly as he had found them. Then, with a last lingering look at the clutch, he took a firm grip on the rope and swung himself free of the ledge. He climbed swiftly, hand over hand, his satisfaction at the success of his mission giving added power to the strength of his arms. The short scramble over the overhang was both painful and arduous, but at last he lay on the short turf of the clifftop, his legs and arms trembling uncontrollably, his breathing ragged and harsh.

He coiled the rope and knocked the stakes from the ground. He was just gathering up the wooden stakes from the headland opposite when he saw the falcon return. She swooped straight into the eyrie, and settled down, totally unaware that anything had changed.

He felt light at heart as he walked back down the hill, even though he realized that while he had ruined the eggs as collectors' items, there was nothing to stop anyone gaining access to the eyrie and perhaps smashing the eggs in rage and frustration on finding them to be useless. Still, he thought there was a good chance that they might desist, because it would be more profitable to return at a later date and try to take the young birds.

Once the eggs were hatched, the chicks, or eyasses, were safe until they were ready to fly. He knew enough about falconry to know that an eyas taken too soon from the eyrie would not prosper. Nor would it train easily, instead spending its days in senseless, hysterical screaming. For the brief time that the eyasses were at risk he could mount a special guard, perhaps persuading one of his bird-watching friends to come and stay on the island and take turns with him in keeping watch. Until then he felt he could relax.

6

The Way of the Egg

The clear skies and bright sunshine of early spring gave way to cloud and rain, as a series of depressions swept in from the Atlantic. Gales were sudden and savage, moving in from the southwest in warm, moist, gusting force to set the sea leaping and foaming against the base of the cliffs, or blowing from the northwest, bringing stinging showers of cold rain to beat against the land.

The peregrines, like the sea birds, were impervious to the cold, and the wind was their ally. In spite of their weight, they merely had to loft their wings to overcome the force of gravity, to become buoyant, free. Riding the invisible currents of the air with effortless grace, they were able to stay aloft for hours on end if need be. They rose, rather than climbed, into the sky, catching the thermals that surged up from the land and hanging themselves in the sky without any more exertion than the merest curve of a wing tip or a slight flexing of their tails. The mighty power of their pectoral muscles was used only for a fraction of the time they spent on the wing—when hunting, or landing, or moving from one air current to the next.

The burden of pregnancy would have been intolerable to a species so finely attuned, so delicately in balance with its environment. So, throughout the millennia, since long before the mammals adopted their slow, earthbound existence, the peregrines, in company with other birds, had produced their kind by way of the egg. They did so, not because they could not adapt. The way of the egg was ancient, but it was successful, phenomenally so, having many advantages over the way of the mammal, which nourished its embryos within its own body.

Each one of Freya's eggs was a miracle of miniaturization, perfectly programmed and timetabled for the pattern of its future life. The germ cell hung suspended in the yolk, a concentrated soup of fats and proteins which would nourish the growing embryo. The yolk was encapsulated in a sac, attached to the shell by twisted cords, so that when Freya moved the egg, the cords could rotate, allowing the germ to rise to the top of the yolk. In turn the yolk was cushioned, insulated, and protected by a layer of albumen, which also prevented the egg from losing moisture through the porous shell.

The shell itself consisted of crystals of calcium carbonate, laid around a network of protein fibers. This arrangement made the egg extremely strong and resistant to ex-

59

ternal pressures, for when compressed, the crystals locked together like the stones in an arch. When the time came for the egg to hatch, a relatively small pressure from inside the shell would cause it to break.

Each egg that Freya laid cooled slightly after laying, and the contents shrank a little, allowing a bubble of air to seep through the shell. This air would be the first the chick would breathe, a tiny reservoir of life in which the chick could exist as it labored to break through the shell.

So, throughout the long days of spring, as Freya sat brooding, each embryo, like a tiny astronaut immured in his spaceship, recapitulated the history of its race, evolving and changing until at last it had reached the stage when it could survive in the harsh and variable environment that lay beyond the shell.

After her first flush of possessive pride, Freya, at first with extreme caution and reluctance, allowed Frika to take his turn at incubation. Frika, a little nervous at assuming such a responsible task, took up his position with exaggerated care, remaining absolutely motionless until Freya returned. His small body barely covered the clutch, but the insulation of his feathers helped retain heat in the eggs, which pressed warm against his thighs. Cramped and uncomfortable, he was always glad to relinquish his post, but each new day, when Freya called her imperious summons, he flapped over to the ledge, to stand with courtly grace as he waited for her to emerge before stepping gingerly into the eyrie.

Freya hunted little during her brief flights of freedom. Instead she spent the time preening, and bathing in the clear cold waters of a spring that welled out of the ground in a small hollow of the cliffs. The falcons drank little, getting all the moisture they needed from the blood and flesh of their prey, and to aid them in eliminating excess salts from their systems they had special secreting glands in their nostrils. All the same, Freya seldom bathed without swallowing a few drops of water.

Refreshed and invigorated, she would then return to the eyrie, frequently with her underskirts still damp from her bath. This did no harm, and indeed the eggs benefited from the moisture and steamy warmth. It helped prevent fluid loss from the egg and preserved the elasticity of the shell.

As the days passed, as the bracken unfolded their tight green fronds, and a purple haze of hyacinth and squill spread their fragrance over the land, Freya grew more reluctant to leave her eggs. Frika, puzzled and perturbed, came daily to the ledge, bobbing and bowing in a vain endeavor to take over his matrimonial duties. Freya sat on, lethargic, unresponsive, as though she were in a state of trance. It was now the fourth week of incubation, and she was in communion with the fully formed embryos, as yet still imprisoned within the eggs. She could feel them move, and she could hear faint sounds, and she knew, with the innate wisdom of her kind, that her vigil was almost at an end.

The chicks were aware too, aware of the flood of warmth that was Freya. They heard the beat of her heart and the soft rustle of feathers as she moved. They could sense light, and this always made them more active, twisting and kicking as though striving to break away from the lifeline that still attached each embryo to its rapidly shrinking yolk. This exercise helped to develop their muscles, so that when the time came the chick would have the strength to break free of the shell.

For most of the time, however, the embryos slept. They needed but a few more days of growth before the way of the egg led them to the gateway of conscious life—the next stage on the road to independent existence—and a full awareness of their environment.

No one came near to molest the eggs. The sea was too rough to have permitted a landing, for even on the days when the wind did not blow, a heavy ground swell brought giant breakers to thud and crash against the base of the cliff or curl in ponderous white plumes before breaking with a thunderous roar upon the stony beach.

The presence of the peregrines on the island in no way deterred sea birds from nesting nearby, and the cliffs were a scene of indecipherable confusion, as thousands of birds congregated in close-packed colonies, breeding pairs sharing the available space with equal numbers of immature birds.

Highest on the cliff were the razorbills and guillemots, but while the razorbill chose to hide its single egg in some crack or crevice, the guillemot laid its egg on an open ledge. Below them nested the fulmars, choosing the bare soil of wider, less precipitous ledges. Below them again, almost within reach of the surging waves, the dainty kittiwakes built their nests of weed. All around, the wary, watchful gulls hovered and soared, ready to pounce in pillage of any unguarded chick or egg.

Chough and raven, jackdaw and dove, all made their homes on the cliff face. A colony of shags, bottle-green fishermen of sardonic countenance, built their untidy nests in a sheltered corner of the cliffs, One, scavenging the flotsam in search of building material, had found the top half of a hot water bottle. This, protruding from beneath the brooding bird, gave a misleading impression of comfort and sanguinity.

Birds came and went. Guillemots whirred upward from the waves. Kittiwakes hovered around their nests, or sat, bill to bill, their eyes closed in silent rapture. Small rafts of birds floated on the sea, swimming, diving, preening, and suddenly taking flight. Amid the squawking and the chattering, the screaming and wailing, anarchy reigned supreme. Eggs were lost, falling from the ledges into the sea, and the bereaved mothers, quietly waiting their chance, stole other eggs from some absent parent. In time the chick might wander away from its foster parent, to be lost in the milling throng. Sooner or later it would be fed by a passing bird, and thus survive.

Yet in spite of the seeming disorder and chaos, each bird was able to recognize its mate and defend its own small breeding territory. In spite of the apparent squalor of the cliffside slums, each individual bird was immaculate, spotless, and free from any taint of the ordure that limed the rocks. For untold centuries this had been the way of the sea birds, and not only had they survived, but they had prospered.

The sea birds had little to fear from the peregrines. To the casual observer, it would seem that there was an easy and inexhaustible supply of food, yet apart from picking the odd straggling razorbill or guillemot from a flock, the falcons worried them little. In every case there was a reason: the black backs and the herring gulls were too big and powerful to be easy prey, the fulmars and petrels were rancid-fleshed, oily and unsavory, while the auks hugged the waves and at the first sign of danger dived below the surface of the sea.

Occasionally, however, discord marred the harmony of cliffside co-existence. Below the eyrie was a small colony of herring gulls, and as always, as one parent brooded the eggs, the other stood on guard or lazily patroled to and fro in front of the cliff. The peregrines were apt to be careless in the disposal of their food remains, often dropping half-eaten carcasses into the waves, and these were instantly pounced upon by the ravenous, scavenging gulls.

One evening, Freya, on one of her rare hunting expeditions, struck and killed a wood pigeon as it flew up from a potato field. The large gray bird was much heavier than the rock doves that abounded on the coast, and Freya flew heavily back to the eyrie, the pigeon clasped firmly in both talons.

As she passed the herring-gull colony, one young bird, hungrier or more foolhardy than the rest, saw she was carrying prey and was suddenly seized with an impulse to mob the falcon, in the hope that she might drop the prize. Had Freya been a buzzard or a heron the idea might have worked. As things were, Freya waited until the gull was almost at her wing tip, and then, shifting her grip on the pigeon, she shook one foot free.

Her talons raked the gull's chest, tearing lose a cloud of feathers and etching a red raw line across the skin. The gull gave a yelp of fear and alarm, and others of his kind, obeying the age old command, flew at once to his aid.

Next moment Freya was weaving and dodging, swooping down almost to sea level, before climbing skyward, skimming the face of the cliff in an effort to throw off her pursuers and win through to the eyrie. Frika, watching from his perch on the ledge, saw her plight and flew to join battle.

Between them they broke through, bulldozing their way through a snowstorm of screaming, shouting gulls, now so incensed with blood lust and mob hysteria that they knew no fear. Freya pitched the corpse of the wood pigeon onto the ledge, and Frika landed near, crouching over it with mantled wings and gazing skyward with eyes that showed no fear, but blazed an anger as cold and calculating as it was merciless. Freya landed beside him.

To the gulls the peregrines no longer posed a threat. They hovered for a moment over the two falcons crouched upon the ledge, shouting their defiance. Then, uncertain what to do next, they began to drift back to the colony. Freya, however, had no intention of letting them get off so lightly. Perhaps if the gulls had not actually invaded her territory, she might have forgotten the matter. Now she had no choice. Her supremacy had been challenged, and order had to be restored. Screaming at the top of her voice, she launched herself off the ledge and flew straight at the nearest gull.

There were seven of them in all, and it took her a little under two minutes to clear them from the sky. She aimed to punish rather than kill. Kicking, swerving, diving, and swooping, she drove them all down, and when at last they all huddled, cowed and shivering, on the nearby cliffs, each one carried the scars of her whipping.

As she flew back in triumph to the ledge, she heard a

strange cry from the headland opposite. Their guardian had watched the entire sequence of events, and now he cheered her victory.

7

Life in the Eyrie

May came, bringing hot sun and showers of warm rain that blessed the soil and dissolved into vapor, leaving behind a thin green mist of growth. The air was heavy with the scent of hawthorn and gorse and fresh sweet grass. The cuckoo called throughout the long day, flitting hawklike along the low stone hedges of the fields. The mornings were loud with birdsong, and in the velvet dusk the grasshopper warblers sang in secret, hidden in the low, tussocky jungle of growth beside the clifftops.

Freya, brooding in the gray light that preceded the dawn, heard the thin piping cry that heralded the hatching of the first chick. She stirred, and answered, crooning encouragement each time the cry was repeated, faint and muffled from inside the shell. Then the tapping began, as the hatching chick pecked and chipped at the chalky walls of its prison.

A small hole appeared in the shell, a hole which grew and widened as the chick, for the first and last time in its life, used the specially adapted egg tooth it had grown to cut itself free. At the same time it kicked and struggled, arching its neck and jerking its body in a convulsive effort to shatter the shell. The hours passed, and from time to time the chick rested, weary after its struggles, only to wake and resume its efforts. Freya waited patiently, making no attempt to help her offspring.

At last a crack appeared in the shell, and from then on the chick made rapid progress, so that in a short while it lay on the bare earth of the eyrie, surrounded by the broken, yolk-stained fragments of the shell, breathing rapidly as it strove to raise its head and stand up. Its plumage of down clung in wet sticky strands to its naked skin and its eyes bulged grotesquely under closed lids. The minutes passed, and with a shuddering heave it stood upright, swaying and weaving. Then, as if suddenly ashamed of its own nakedness and ugliness, it crawled under the protective wing of Freya.

When the chick emerged, her down had dried and whitened, fluffing out to form a warm, insulating coat, and that evening she took her first feed, succulent slivers of flesh from the breast of a skylark, brought to the eyrie by Frika.

Twenty-four hours later her sister kicked and clawed her way into the world, and on the third day their brother joined them. He was smaller than his sisters, and indeed, from the moment of conception, when his sex was decreed, his needs had been determined and adjusted accordingly. The yolk on which his developing germ was nourished was smaller, and hence the egg was proportionately reduced in size.

In order to survive, the tiercel had to battle for every meal in competition with his older, heavier sisters. Fortunately, he was extremely active and lively, with a wiry strength that was to stand him in good stead in the jostling that took place each mealtime.

For the first few days Freya rarely left the eyrie. The young eyasses still needed the warmth of her body, and they slept for long periods nestled beneath her, waking to instant hunger whenever Frika arrived at the eyrie, bearing the partly plucked carcass of a bird. Frantic with greed and excitement, they snatched and pulled at the warm flesh that Freya hurriedly carved for them, their high-pitched yelping cries dying away to throaty gurgles as their crops gradually filled. Replete, they shuffled away, dozing together in a warm huddle of contentment, as Freya demolished the remainder of the meal.

During this time Frika willingly accepted his role as breadwinner, for to hunt was joy and life to him. It needed no effort of will on his part, no sense of determination or drive. He did not even need the stimulus of hunger. Perched on a high ledge, or soaring above the cliffs, he was ever watchful, ever on the alert for further victims. His eyesight was so keen that he could identify a rock dove two miles distant, and though he did not always launch an attack, the sight never failed to arouse the instincts of the hunter. Crouched and tense, he would watch the progress

of the unsuspecting bird with an unswerving concentration that did not relax until the dove was out of sight.

Another breadwinner was Larus, the black-backed gull, whose mate had just hatched three chicks in their great messy nest of heather and seaweed. The gulls had built their nest behind a high stack of rock at the top of the cliff, less than a hundred yards from the peregrine eyrie, but though the falcons barked a warning whenever Larus strayed too near, they tended to ignore the gulls, and Larus, for his part, steered clear of the peregrines, although he was bigger and heavier than Freya herself.

Larus had no friends, and no near neighbors. When the broad shadow of his wings passed over the cliffs, the herring-gull chicks pressed close to the shielding rocks, and the oyster catcher piped an urgent warning to her young. Larus was a killer, a robber of eggs and a stealer of chicks, and even the adults among the smaller sea birds feared his great snapping bill. Larus killed messily, slapping and slamming and shaking his victims about until they died, or could move no more, before skinning them or gulping them down whole into his ravenous maw.

Once, he and his kind had been mercifully few, but during the past century their numbers had increased ten fold. There were many reasons for this population explosion. Marksmen no longer roamed the shores, as they had done at the turn of the century, shooting sea gulls for sport. Gulls' eggs, once considered a delicacy, were now regarded as not worth risking life and limb to collect. So the gulls enjoyed immunity from attack, and the expanding fishing fleets around the coasts provided an everlasting flow of fresh offal to feed their growing numbers. Inland, near every town and city, the growing heaps of garbage created fresh foraging grounds. The gulls were not fussy about what they ate.

It was to the garbage dump that Larus made his leisurely way one blustery Monday morning. Long experience had taught him that on this day tons of edible refuse found their way to the dump, following the orgy of eating and waste that took place every weekend, and countless plates were scraped into the dustbins that stood outside every hotel and cafe and private house. Larus knew little of the ways of men, but he knew more about the sanitary arrangements of the city than did most of the human occupants.

The dump was already crowded when Larus arrived. A cloud of herring gulls flickered white around the bulldozer, already busy leveling and burying the latest load of waste. A group of starlings bustled busily over the bare brown earth in the wake of the bulldozer, goose-stepping here and there as they snatched crumbs of offal from the soil. A cock chaffinch, his breast blushing pink, seized a morsel of bread and carried it off to his young. Two crows hammered and pulled at the uncooked carcass of a chicken.

Larus planed down and landed amid a litter of paper, plastic, and empty food cans. He found bread crusts, bacon rinds, a roast potato, a slice of ham. Soon his crop was bulging, and he grew more selective in his choice of food, choosing only the daintier morsels of waste. A half-empty can of cat food, pink and fishy, caught his eye, and he emptied it in three beak loads, spilling a third of it on the

73

ground. He stood for a moment, his webbed feet slipping and sliding among the debris, waiting for the contents of his crop to settle.

Among the citizens of Saint David's was a housewife both conscientious and methodical. The dustmen knew that when they came to empty her dustbin it would be as clean inside as it was out, smelling of pine disinfectant, with its contents nearly wrapped and packaged. She rarely used canned food, preferring to buy fresh, but this weekend she had opened a large can of peaches. As always, she had rinsed the can, and then carefully pushed the lid, with its sharp serrated edge, inside the can. She had a horror of anyone cutting himself on the sharp metal.

The can now lay on the dump, its lid tucked away inside but still hinged by a scrap of metal. Larus stood on the can, felt his foot slide over the polished surface of the lid and slip inside. The lid sprang back and trapped his foot in the can. He shook his foot hard and felt the first stab of pain as the edge of the lid nicked his skin.

Startled, he spread his wings in flight, and the wind gripped the can like a sail, throwing him off balance and making him fly harder. His efforts rocked the can, and the edge sawed away at his leg. The bulldozer driver saw his struggles and grinned to himself. He had no love for the gulls.

Herring gulls watched Larus's drunken flight and circled around, mobbing him, as was their custom with anything strange to them. Larus threw up the contents of his crop in order to lighten his load, and the herring gulls followed the noisome mess as it fell to earth.

Larus wore the can for eighteen hours, moping disconsolately by the cliff. Each time he moved, the lid sawed a little farther through his leg, disarticulating it at the joint. It bled for a while, weakening him still further, so that when he tried to fly his wings were too weary to carry him far. He planed down to the sea, and the can filled with water.

He felt easier floating on the sea. He bathed a little and sipped some of the sea water. Then he tried to rise. The waterlogged can held him fast, and he struggled in vain to lift himself off the surface of the sea. Beneath him the can had sliced through his leg, so that now a mere fragment of skin held the foot in place. Next time Larus tried to fly, the sliver of skin snapped, and the can sank slowly down to the sea bed, followed by a shoal of small pouting. Later the crabs found the foot and tore it to shreds, eating all save the bones.

Larus was free, but he was lame. The antiseptic action of the salt water soon healed his stump, and as the days went by he learned to balance and to alight on one leg without pitching ignominiously on to his beak, wings asprawl on the turf. But he was slower, less agile, and an easy target for irate parents when he went raiding a colony of herring gulls. The garbage dump was still a fruitful source of food, but associated with it was the memory of the sharp, stinging pain that had been the cause of all his trouble. For many weeks he avoided the place.

June arrived, and the long period of unsettled weather came to an end as a vast anticyclone deepened and intensified over land and sea. Each day the sun blazed from a cloudless sky, and the land soaked up the heat, drawing fresh cool winds from the sea. Each evening the wind died, and the night air was calm and cool as the stars glittered in the cold canopy of the sky.

Frika hunted during the day, but he was especially active at dawn and dusk. The first light of day found the eyasses awake and querulous with hunger, and their yelping cries did not abate until they were satiated with food. Prey was so plentiful and easy to obtain that Frika had no difficulty in keeping up with the demands of the youngsters, frequently bringing food to the eyrie, only to be greeted with studied indifference by the youngsters, still stupefied and somnolent from the remains of their last feed.

At such times Frika either ate his catch himself, or stored the carcass in a convenient crevice on the cliff face. Then the next time the calls for food echoed from the eyrie, all he had to do was to visit his larder to produce an instant meal. This led to a considerable amount of waste, for carcasses which had laid in the sun too long were rejected and dropped in the sea. Many lay forgotten on the cliffs, left to moulder and rot, to break down into the elements from which they sprang.

Larus soon discovered that the untidy and wasteful housekeeping of the peregrines could be turned to his advantage, and he took to hanging about on the sea beneath the eyrie, paddling with his one leg and waiting for the carcasses that fell from the sky. His bulk, plus the fact that he was always on the spot, meant that the swooping herring gulls who hoped to share the plunder were invariably disappointed. Larus always got to the booty first, and there was no one courageous enough to challenge his right.

Before very long Larus, not content with scavenging, began to plunder the peregrines' larder. He chose his moments carefully, waiting until both birds were away from the eyrie and then drifting quietly along the side of the cliff in the short intervals of their absences. As soon as he had snatched and swallowed his prize, he returned to the safety of the sea, there to digest his ill-gotten meal.

The eyasses were growing apace, and Freya was able to leave them for long periods to join Frika in his hunting forays or to perch on a ledge in the sun, attending in meticulous detail to a toilet that had been over neglected of late.

Now over a fortnight old, the young peregrines were beginning to develop distinct personalities. Iya, the eldest, was placid and complacent. Wayee, her sister, was more aggressive and belligerent, quick to seize the best portions of food and scream defiance at any attempts to deprive her of her prize. Chek, the tiercel, small and lively, seemed to need less sleep than his sisters, and often, as they dozed the long hours away, Chek spent the time pattering round the eyrie, poking into shadowy corners, snapping at the flies that buzzed around his head, or toying idly with the ragged remains of a jackdaw's wing that lay among the debris.

The ledge in front of the eyrie grew daily more untidy, and flies swarmed amid the litter of past feasts. Added to the mess were the castings, or pellets, of the falcons, the indigestible remains of bone and feather which their crops could not digest and which they threw up after each feed.

Early one morning, as his parents were quartering the cliffs to the north of the island, Chek wandered out of the eyrie and began to explore the ledge that lay outside. To the left the narrow shelf of rock terminated abruptly in a vertical drop to the sea below, and Chek peered down, watching the soft breathing of the ocean as it rose and fell, thudding into the cave below and emerging with a soft sigh.

A cold breeze wafted up the cliff face, stirring Chek's downy plumage and making him shiver. He retreated back along the ledge, past the mouth of the eyrie and along the cliff face, moving slightly downward. He stopped, and was about to return to the eyrie, when a movement caught his eye. Ahead of him a bunch of sea pinks nodded their heads above the soft green cushion of their foliage, and to one of the blossoms clung a white feather.

It was this feather, waving in the breeze, that had caught Chek's attention. Now it waved again, beckoning and enticing, and Chek stalked along the ledge until at last he could pounce. Grasping the feather in his talon, he turned to make his way back along the ledge. A rush of wings made him look up, expecting to see his mother returning with food. Instead, perched on the ledge and blocking his way back to the eyrie, stood Larus the lame, his yellow eye glinting hungrily, his great bill, splashed with vivid red, open in anticipation.

Chek fell backward, his talons spread wide in the age-old defense position of the birds of prey. The wind took his feather and carried it away. Larus watched it go, turning over and over in the wind and rising above the cliff before sinking slowly down to the waves. Then he turned uncertainly back to Chek. This was no helpless herring-gull chick, but a black-eyed ball of fury, spitting and hissing like a snake. Tentatively, Larus reached forward, seeking to grab Chek with the very tip of his beak. Chek kicked out, and his talons raked the gull's head.

Larus jumped back and shook himself. He was growing increasingly nervous, for he knew that at any moment the falcons might return. He was determined to make one last attempt. A sudden lunge, and a quick flick of his beak, and Chek would go spinning out into mid-air, to fall into the sea. There Larus could devour him at his leisure.

At that moment Frika hit him, and the force of the blow pinned him to the ledge, splintering one wing and tearing a great flap of skin from his neck. Larus tore himself free and launched himself into space, one wing frantically fanning the air as he spiraled down to the waves. Freya came up from below, hit him hard, and swooped past, turning to drop and hit him again. Larus was already dead, his head half-severed from his body.

For some time Freya and Frika hovered and wheeled above the corpse, until at last, waterlogged and sodden, it was pitched up on the shore by the waves. There, later, the herring gulls found it, and eventually they managed to break it up. As the dusk came Chek dozed in the safety of the eyrie, huddled against his sisters for warmth.

8

Cree's Hunting

Throughout the ages, those species survived which were best able to adapt to a changing environment. The animals and birds which colonized Britain after the retreat of the last ice age enjoyed a long era of peace and prosperity. For thousands of years the environment changed little, and such changes as did take place occurred slowly, giving all forms of life time to adjust their ways accordingly. Then, suddenly, all was changed, as the dawn of the industrial revolution began to bring about alterations as swift as they were dramatic.

Such alterations were manmade, and so it followed that the species which were to flourish were those best able to adapt to the ways of man. The house fly, the rat, and the sparrow learned quickly. They came to dine and shared in the leavings of the most wasteful and destructive species ever to inhabit the earth. Others learned too. The herring gull was equally at home nesting on cliff ledges or the rooftops of seaside houses, and it fed its young on fish offal thrown from the trawlers, edible refuse from the garbage dumps, or worms turned by the farmer's plow. Some species prospered. Others declined.

The rabbit prospered, for the pattern of British agriculture might have been expressly designed to conserve the rabbit. Acres of grass and grain, in small fields bounded by miles of dry, well-drained hedge banks in which to burrow, and interspersed with small areas of copse and heathland, overgrown with thickets of briar and bramble, made an ideal habitat.

Each evening, as the air grew calm and still, and the sun sank beyond the scattered islands to the west, the rabbits emerged to crop the short sweet turf of the headlands. For centuries they had infested the island, and once they had been regarded as a valuable crop, a welcome harvest for a people who were often short of meat.

Like the pigeon, the rabbit fell from favor as a table delicacy, and as the demand for rabbit meat dropped, so its value declined until it was not worth harvesting. So the rabbit population thrived, and soon began to impoverish the farmland. Each winter the farmer spent many hours snaring and ferreting the burrows, but the value of the catch provided little return for his efforts, and each summer their legions seemed as numerous as ever.

Only the birds benefited from the rabbits. Owl and sparrow hawk, buzzard and raven, crow and gull, all flocked to the feast, for now the thickets of fern and heather swarmed with succulent youngsters fresh from the nest. Even the peregrines took rabbits, especially when rain and gales made birds reluctant to fly.

One evening, Bayoo the buzzard drifted across the Sound from the mainland. He had spent over an hour waiting for the tide to deposit the carcass of a guillemot on the shore, only to be robbed at the last moment by a black-backed gull, which swooped down and plucked the dead sea bird from the waves.

Although larger than the gull, the buzzard knew better than to dispute ownership of the prize, so he had come to the island in the hope of finding a rabbit. Now he hung in the air, fifty feet above the heather, his great talons opening and closing as his eyes scanned the ground, watching for the slightest movement.

A hundred yards away Cree the kestrel also hunted for his supper. Although dwarfed by the massive size and wingspread of the buzzard, the tiny falcon paid him no heed. Like the buzzard, he hung above the moor, his tail spread and his long, pointed wings fanned the air as he hovered in the sky. He hoped for mice or voles, but he was on the alert for any movement that would betray the presence of life.

A fern nodded when all should have been still. Bayoo swept over to the spot in a scything arc and hung, watching. A young rabbit was grazing the short grass beneath a gorse bush, but the prickly spines of the gorse prevented Bayoo from dropping on his prey. Inch by slow inch, the rabbit moved forward out of cover. The buzzard waited, tense, expectant.

A field mouse ran up a heather stem, and the kestrel dropped in a long slanting dive that took him within a few feet of the ground. The mouse ran back and disappeared from view into a tunnel beneath the heather, and Cree swept away to resume his vigil. A lizard slid off a rock and moved swiftly over the dense wiry turf. Cree pounced, his talons closed, and the lizard, still writhing and twisting, was dismembered and swallowed. The kestrel sat hunched on a tussock of grass, brooding as the tail of the lizard slowly disappeared into his crop. Then he rose into the air and resumed his watching.

The rabbit had left the shelter of the gorse bush, and was now feeding in the open, but within a yard of it lay the open mouth of a burrow. Bayoo closed the gap between himself and his prey and waited again, aware that if he struck too soon the rabbit would gain sanctuary before he had a chance to sink his talons home.

A thousand feet above the island, the peregrines waited. Far away across the Sound a pigeon beat its way homeward, its crop laden with food, and instantly the falcons were ready, and watchful. Frika changed his station, dropping three hundred feet and moving half a mile to the east, ready to intercept the pigeon, and, if need be, drive it up toward Freya.

With a low drone, a cockchafer beetle flew ponderously over the heather. It tried to alight on a bracken stem, fell off, and rolled into the heather, its legs waving clumsily as it tried to turn right side up. Cree saw, and the cockchafer joined the lizard in his crop.

The rabbit had moved away from the burrow, but something had alarmed it. It stood alert, uneasy, its ears raised as it listened. Until it lowered its head and resumed feeding Bayoo dared not strike. Still he waited, motionless in the warm air.

The pigeon had spotted Frika, and turned, flying faster and climbing toward the island. Freya watched, waited, and when she judged that the time and distance were right, closed her wings, clenched her talons tight to her chest, and fell.

In mid-stoop she peeled off and flew rapidly back across the island, screaming loudly to Frika. Even in the act of killing, her sharp eyes had noticed a slight movement on the cliff above the eyrie, and sensing danger, she had abandoned the pigeon. The safety of the eyasses came first.

The intruder on the cliff was a collie dog from the farm, who had sneaked away in the hope of catching a rabbit. He posed no threat to the eyasses, and indeed, was not even aware of the existence of the peregrines until Freya struck him a violent blow on the side of the head. He leaped sideways with a snarling growl, snapping at Freya as she swooped again. Next moment Frika was harrying him from the rear, both birds whirling and diving, screaming their fury until, bemused and buffeted by the din, the dog fled back along the cliff, barking loudly as he went.

The rabbit went too, vanishing in a flicker of brown fur the instant the uproar started. In a last vain attempt to secure his supper the buzzard dropped, landing claws asprawl and grasping empty earth at the very entrance to the burrow. He flapped away and circled the island once before flying off into the gathering dusk.

Cree followed. Another cockchafer had been added to the contents of his crop, and now, comfortably full, he flew back to his eyrie on the mainland cliffs. The pigeon was already at roost, her head sunk deep in her shoulders. She had forgotten, if in fact she was ever really aware, that violent death had missed her by seconds. The night deepened, and in the peregrine eyrie the grumbling of the hungry eyasses gradually subsided in sleep.

The youngsters were now over three weeks old and fast replacing their baby plumage with feathers. Their heads were quite dark, and their breasts were beginning to feather, while on their backs two narrow bands formed the shape of a figure eight. They spent a great deal of time pulling and worrying at their plumage and flapping their wings amid the crumbling remains of feather and bone that littered the eyrie, sending clouds of dusty white down floating up into the air and over the cliff.

Their appetites were more voracious than ever, and every hour or so they clamored to be fed. The speed of their growth, and the demands of their developing plumage, called for plentiful supplies of minerals and vitamins. These they got from the feathers and bones as well as from the meat of the carcasses they were brought.

Pigeon continued to appear regularly on the menu, together with blackbirds, skylarks, rock pipits, and an occasional jackdaw or lapwing. Sometimes Freya brought a guillemot or a shearwater, lugging the heavy corpse back to the eyrie with wildly flapping wings. Each mealtime was a jostling, stamping, shoving match, accompanied by shrill screams from the youngsters, cries which gradually died away to throaty gurgles as the carcass was dismembered and lumps of meat thrust down the most readily available crop.

By dawn, the demands of the three eyasses who had gone supperless to bed were so urgent and insistent that long before the bees began to work among the tall spires of the foxgloves that towered above the spreading fern, Frika slipped off the ledge and flew northward and west, out over the sea. A mile and a half away a pinnacle of rock loomed a hundred feet above the waves, and hugging the face of the cliff, Frika swept around the island, surprising a small black and white sea bird that flew toward the clifftop on rapidly whirring wings.

Frika kicked out, clutching the bird across the back, paralyzing it so that it died almost instantaneously. In giving its last scream it opened its enormous, vari-colored beak and dropped its load of small silver fish, eighteen in all, which fell in a shimmering rain down into the sea. Long before the fish sank beneath the waves, they were seized and swallowed by a herring gull and a fulmar, who fought over the last fish and succeeded in tearing it in half.

Frika bore the dead puffin back to the eyrie, and within fifteen minutes all that remained on the ledge were the wings and the head, with its massive, clownlike beak of vermillion, gold, and gray. One pink webbed foot had still to disappear into Wayee's crop and hung like a grotesque swollen tongue from her half-open beak. Chek attempted to pull it away and got a hearty kick for his pains. Retiring to a safe distance, Chek found the head of the puffin and tried to swallow it, unsuccessfully, whereupon he shook it, and the head flew from his grasp and tumbled over the ledge, down into the sea. For a long time it floated, like a gaudily colored buoy, until the waves took it and cast it up on the shore. It lay for several days among the weed and

86

flotsam, providing many a meal for the small denizens of the tideline, and finally ᴛne empty skull became a home for a colony of sandhoppers.

Once the puffins had swarmed on Ramsey in the thousands, returning each spring after a winter wandering the Atlantic ocean, to share their clifftop burrows with the rabbits. The relationship was not entirely harmonious, and many a rabbit was evicted from her rightful home by painful nips from the puffin's sharp bill. Each species survived, however, and did the other no real harm.

Then the rats came to Ramsey. Whether they stowed away in some cargo and escaped after being landed on the island or whether they swam ashore from one of the frequent shipwrecks around the coast is not known. One thing is certain—man was the unwitting cause of their presence. As always, the rats prospered and bred, and the fate of the puffins was sealed, for although the rats did not molest the adult birds, they took the eggs and butchered the young birds in the burrows when the parents were away. Each spring fewer and fewer puffins arrived, until at last they came to nest on Ramsey no more.

Only a few pairs nested on the North Bishop, where Frika had killed his bird. Their last great stronghold on the Welsh coast lay at Skomer, the island to the south of Saint Bride's bay. Even here their numbers were decreasing. Oil pollution took its toll, as adult birds far out to sea surfaced to find themselves enmeshed in the clinging, suffocating slime of an oil slick. Black-backed gulls haunted the puffinries and slaughtered adults and chicks indiscriminately.

Occasionally, it seemed, the puffin was its own worst enemy. Far to the west lay the island of Grassholm, and here in the late nineteenth century the puffins thronged by the hundreds of thousands. The thick green thatch of turf proved ideal for their burrows, but gradually the puffins so undermined the fescue grass that it dried out and died, and the labyrinthine network of burrows crumbled and eroded away.

The puffins left, never to return. Instead, the island was colonized by gannets, which over the years grew to such numbers that their droppings bleached the island white. On a clear day the island could be seen from Ramsey, its snowy crown shimmering in unearthly splendor in the sun.

Perhaps this was the natural way of the sea birds. Perhaps it was part of a long, slow cycle, whereby the puffin, like man, destroyed the environment on which he depended by sheer weight of numbers, only to desert it and leave it for another species to colonize and restore. Perhaps one day the gannets would depart, and on the rich guano deposits the grass would grow anew, laying down a thick mat of turf for the puffins to repopulate. We may not know, for the answers to these riddles are lost in the misty realms of time, and the sea keeps its secrets well.

9

The Bird Fancier

Of all the birds of prey the kestrel alone had some success in learning to live with man, to adjust its ways to a rapidly changing environment. Raptors and falcons by right of their hooked, notched beaks and long pointed wings, they survived, and even flourished, while other predators gradually declined in number. Over mountain and moorland, clifftop and heathland, farmland, fen, and parkland, they picked a frugal living whenever the opportunity presented itself. Farmers came to welcome the sight of a kestrel hovering over a fallow field, knowing that its diet consisted mainly of mice, voles, and harmful insects.

Like the peregrines, the kestrels built no nests, but they were more adaptable in their choice of site. A hollow tree trunk, or an abandoned crow's nest, was just as acceptable as an eyrie on some crumbling cliff. They even nested in cities, and in London one pair successfully raised a brood on a ledge high above the House of Parliament.

They were quick to discover new hunting grounds—disused airports, industrial sites, playing fields, and railway embankments. As each new multi-lane highway was built, the kestrels learned to exploit the potential offered by the great ribbon of concrete and were seen hovering over the grassy embankments on either side of the speedways.

Some kestrels did not need to adapt and clung to the age-old ways of their ancestors, living on in the more remote, wilder regions where the impact of man had had little or no effect. Such a bird was Cree, who with his mate and three hungry youngsters shared an eyrie high on a ledge on the crumbling slate cliffs to the south of the mainland. He knew little of the ways of man until chance, and a high wind, carried him over the walls and into the grounds of an old house three miles from the sea.

For two days the wind had blown a gale, bringing driving rain in shimmering gray sheets across the angry sea, ripping through the growing corn, setting all in turmoil and confusion, and saturating the living landscape with an all-pervading moisture that clung to every grass blade, every twig and leaf and fern.

Gulls and rooks beat slowly over the land, hedgehopping in order to miss the worst fury of the blasts. Blackbirds and thrushes skulked in the thickets of gorse, flying only when necessary, and then only for a few yards. Insects and small rodents hid themselves away, sheltering below the thick

90

thatch of turf that grew upon the cliffs or hiding in count-less nooks and crannies in the rocks and dry stone walls.

Cree went hungry. To hover was impossible, and even to quarter the ground in the teeth of such buffeting proved unsuccessful, and pointless because of the lack of prey. He turned inland, seeking the shelter of the wooded valleys that wound their secret way over the drab, flat landscape. Even here the all-pervading rain drove every potential quarry under cover, and so Cree came to the garden.

The owner of the house was an old man, a recluse. Until he retired he had lived all his life in a city. Now he kept birds—rare pheasants and parakeets, ornamental waterfowl and pigeons. He kept them not out of love for their beauty or fascination with their ways but because of a preoccupa-tion with the bizarre, the unusual. His main interest lay in breeding rarities and show birds so that he could enjoy the vicarious pleasure of winning prizes with his exhibits.

He kept pigeons—Birmingham Rollers and Flying Tip-plers. The rollers were originally bred in the town of Birmingham, and their tumbling ability was so highly de-veloped that they would climb to a great altitude and then spin back to earth in a lightning swift succession of somer-saults, leveling out just above the ground. The tipplers had lost their ability to tumble but were renowned for their stamina, being able to stay aloft for hours at a time.

The pigeons were kept in a loft on the roof of the house and were allowed the freedom of the garden so that they could supplement their diet of corn with weed seeds and young greenstuffs. Some weeks ago Frika had sighted one of the rollers as he harried a rock dove over the farmland to the north, and intrigued by the curious rolling fall of the tame bird, he had abandoned his quarry and sped over to the house, killing the roller in full view of the old man and leaving a trail of blood and feathers across the lawn. It had been an isolated incident on Frika's part, and he promptly forgot the house and the odd behavior of the pigeon.

The old man did not forget, and for a while he kept his pigeons shut in the loft while he watched anxiously to see if the peregrine would return. He did not own a gun, although he would not have hesitated to use it if he had. He knew nothing of the wild birds protection act and did not recognize Frika as a peregrine. To him all hawks were vermin, to be destroyed without compunction before they murdered too many of his feathered possessions.

The old man fed his captive birds well, too well, and much of the grain and corn soured or sprouted among the unkempt flowerbeds and shrubberies in the grounds. This waste food attracted rats and mice, which bred in the stables and outhouses and grew fat and sleek on the food the birds left to waste. Soon they grew bold, and not content with coming out at night to clear up the leavings, they began to appear in broad daylight, scurrying bright-eyed and eager among the pecking birds. From time to time they took eggs and young birds from the nests of the waterfowl on the lake, and although the old man set traps and laid poison in the outhouses, he could do little to control their numbers. A few cats would soon have solved his problem for him, but these he dared not keep.

So, on this wet and windy morning, Cree found what seemed to be an ideal hunting ground. He caught two mice in quick succession and carried them to the top of a dead tree, where he perched on the sawed-off stump of a branch to dismember and swallow his prey. Then he surprised a short-tailed vole at the foot of the very tree on which he perched. He dropped on it and bore it away out of the shelter of the wooded garden and over the windswept fields to the eyrie. One vole did not go far among his hungry youngsters, so he returned once more to the garden, and this time the old man saw him as he swooped low over the lawn.

He did not see the kestrel carry off a young rat, nor did he know about the two mice and the vole that Cree had already taken. He felt sure that what he had seen was a return of the same hawk that had stolen one of his prize pigeons. Now he kept closer watch, and the following day he saw Cree perching on the dead stump, watching the ground for signs of movement. The gale had blown itself out, dying as suddenly as it had erupted, and now a warm sun made the air humid as it dried the moisture out of the ground.

Cree could now have returned to his old hunting grounds, but having found such a plentiful supply of food he was reluctant to abandon it. He paid several visits to the garden that day and never once returned to the eyrie without a full crop and food for the young kestrels dangling from his talons.

That evening the old man went into one of the outhouses, and from the dark recesses under a bench he pulled out an old chest. Impatiently he brushed off the worst of the dust and the cobwebs and pried open the lid, rummaging around until he found what he was seeking. He carried it over to the window and examined it closely. It was a trap, small and light, of a curious half-moon shape, its jaws now stiff with rust and disuse.

The old man got to work with the oil can and a wire brush, and soon the trap was restored to its original efficiency. When set, it lay on the bench, its jaws spread in a circle. The old man touched the center plate, ever so gently, with a screwdriver, and the jaws snapped shut. Nodding with satisfaction, he carried it out into the garden and laid it at the foot of the dead stump. Then he fetched a ladder and a hammer and a stout staple and very carefully he set the trap on the flat surface of the stump, securing the chain to the trunk of the tree with the staple. Dusk was falling as he put away his tools and retired indoors.

Night came, mild and dry, with low clouds drifting over the face of the moon, so that the shadows under the trees seemed to come alive, now fading, then materializing, like phantoms of the past, struggling to regain an earthly existence. A dark shape detached itself from an elm and drifted past the house. In the undergrowth small shapes moved, scurrying and rustling through the dry leaves.

On noiseless wings the owl swept once more over the lawn, listening with large, offset ears that could locate with pinpoint accuracy the slightest sound. Once he swooped on a young rat, but the treacherous moon betrayed his presence at the last moment and the rat escaped. The owl swooped up, and closing his wings, alighted on top of the stump.

There was a dry, metallic click and the crunch of breaking bones. Held by both shanks, the owl screamed and flapped his wings in anguish. For a moment he hung in the air, frantic with fear and pain as he tried to fly away from the thing that gripped him. The chain held fast. The trap slid from the top of the stump and fell, dragging the owl down.

From time to time during the night the owl made fresh attempts to struggle free. Each effort grew a little weaker, and the jaws of the trap bit deeper into the skin and sinew between the broken bones, lacerating and tearing the living flesh, until at last the blood vessels of the legs gave way. The spirit of the owl faded into the shadows of the night, and only his lifeless corpse hung from the stump.

At first light the old man hurried over to the stump, thinking he had caught his hawk, but when he saw the large head and reproachful brown eyes of the owl he tore the corpse down and flung it on the rubbish heap in disgust. Resetting the trap, he reflected that all was not lost. The trap had been tested and proved, the garden had been rid of one more pest, and it was yet very early in the day. He still stood a good chance of catching the hawk.

Cree left the ledge where he had spent the night, circled the eyrie once, and flew confidently away. His mate crouched low, brooding her young in the chill of the early dawn. Noon passed, and dusk fell over the tall cliffs. The stars shone, and all seemed as it was before, but Cree did not return. He hung head-down from the stump in the garden, and the stars had gone out of his eyes.

The old man, his birds, and the rats and mice were left in peace. Soon the rats gained access to the house and larder, and six months later an apparently healthy rat contaminated some ham with a drop of its urine. The old man ate the ham, not knowing that it had been soiled, or that it now contained the spirochetes that were the cause of infectious jaundice. Soon the first nausea and sickness overtook him, and his temperature began to rise.

After his death, his birds were destroyed, and the rats were exterminated with poison. The house stood empty and derelict, and the following spring another pair of owls took up residence in the garden.

10

The Raid on the Eyrie

The glaring heat of the summer afternoon hung like a pall over the island. No breeze came to stir the rhythmic swell of the sea, and on the ledge outside the eyrie the full-fledged eyasses dozed, beaks agape, wings spread wide to catch any stray current of cooling air. Freya and Frika perched in deepest shade, each engrossed in attending with meticulous detail to the lengthy process of preening.

By far the most important part of this daily ritual was the careful combing of the flight and tail feathers, for it was upon the efficiency of these that the bird depended for its powers of flight, whether in pursuit of prey or escape from danger. Each vaned feather was a masterpiece of intricate engineering, consisting of a hollow shaft, or quill, from both sides of which grew a series of barbs. Each barb was in itself a miniature feather, carrying on its central spine a series of hooked barbules. Each barbule in turn locked onto a row of unhooded barbules on the neighboring barb. Thus each vaned feather could withstand a considerable buffeting, and if, as happened with each flight, some of the barbules became unhooked, the defect could soon be remedied.

The preening process, and the frequent ruffling of feathers that accompanied it, disturbed the blood-sucking parasites that lived among the insulating layers of inner down feathers. Their scurrying movements irritated the falcons, causing them to scratch vigorously at their polls with their curved talons. Each falcon carried its quota of these unwelcome guests, and already the eyasses were infested with them. Yet in the main the parasites caused little harm, and the birds remained healthy in spite of them.

Preoccupied with their preening, the falcons paid little heed to the low throb of diesel engines, as a fishing boat slid slowly past the cliffs and came to anchor off the beach of Abawr Mawr. Boats were a familiar sight to the peregrines, and after a sudden sharp stare of inquiry, they ignored the vessel. The harsh rattle of the anchor chain died away, and silence descended once more. The boat floated on the glassy surface of the sea, rising and falling with a gentle, easy sway.

A man sat in the stern of the boat, studying the cliff through a powerful pair of binoculars. The twin black orbs passed disinterestedly over the nesting guillemots and kittiwakes and ignored the brooding fulmars. They swung skyward, climbing the cliffs and scanning every ledge, until at last they stopped, immobile, focused on the peregrine eyrie. Chek, roused by a fly that buzzed around his head, caught the flash of sunlight on the lens and paused to gaze seaward.

A few minutes later the boat moved away. It passed south of the island and was lost in the shimmering haze that hung over Saint Bride's bay. It was evening before it reached port, a tiny harbor on the south coast of the county. The man moored his boat and then took pencil and paper from a locker. Leaning on the engine cowling, he hastily scribbled a note: "Your inquiry about peregrines to hand. I know of only one eyrie, the young ready to leave any day now."

The writer paused a moment, his pencil poised above the page. Then a slow smile spread over his features as he wrote on: "I have already had one offer, of fifty pounds per bird. If you feel you can better this price, meet me in the bar of the Bristol Trader, tomorrow at noon. I shall be seated under the clock."

He folded the note and sealed it in an envelope. Then he clambered out of the boat and up onto the harbor, making his way along the quay to where a large yacht lay moored, its gleaming white paintwork rose-hued by the rays of the setting sun. As he set foot on the gangplank a burly sailor appeared, barring his way. Without a word he handed over the letter and, turning, made his way out of the harbor and up into the town.

The bar of the Bristol Trader was shady and cool, and the elderly Italian shivered as he stepped in out of the hot

glare of the midday sun. His was the white yacht in the harbor. In addition he owned a villa on the Italian coast, a town house in Paris, and a private plane. He had come a long way since the war and his early deals in the black market. Now, although his financial affairs would not bear too close a scrutiny, he could afford to buy off those who threatened him, and he was free to indulge his lifelong passion, birds of prey. In his villa he kept an aviary, a large and valuable collection of eagles, owls, falcons, and hawks, many of which were trained to fly from his wrist. His enemies, and they were many, called him *Il Avvoltoio*, the vulture. He knew, and did not care.

He approached the man seated in the bar. "I received your note, Mr. Smith. May I offer you some refreshment?"

Tinker Smith half-rose from his chair, and his dark eyes glimmered in amusement. "You speak better English than I do, Mr. Rossetti. Still, that's not surprising I suppose, since Welsh is my mother tongue. I'll take a brandy, if it's no trouble."

They sat in silence for a while, Tinker crouched over his glass, his squat, powerful form immobile, his eyes never leaving the Italian's face. Rossetti, fingertips together, stared at the surface of the table. "There is the question of your British Customs officer," he began softly. "I must have clearance before I sail for Italy, and the birds must not be on board then."

"Easy," shrugged Tinker, "and all the better for me. With my reputation I wouldn't be too happy bringing the birds ashore, not even for an hour or two. We'll rendezvous out at sea, and do the transfer then. What about the price?"

"I thought seventy-five," murmured Rossetti, studying his fingernails.

"Each?" queried Tinker.

The Italian nodded. "When will I know the trip is on?"

Tinker grinned. "The morning you wake and see my boat is missing from its berth. Any day now, if the weather holds. Now, look at this map. Here's where we'll meet. Say, eleven A.M."

The days remained fine, but with the nights mist came, rolling in great white cotton wool clouds from the sea, veiling the moon and muffling all sound, clinging tenaciously to turf and moss and rock and stone, lingering until long after dawn. In the wan gray light the eyasses shivered and huddled together for warmth as the mist first condensed and coated their plumage with silver lace and finally congealed into an all-pervading wetness that darkened their feathers and left them bedraggled. Later the sun came, and the eyasses flapped their wings in a fine rainbow of spray before stretching themselves and sprawling in the luxury of warmth and light.

For three nights the weather continued thus, but on the fourth a fresh breeze kept the fog at bay. That evening Owen Thomas lingered on the cliffs until long after dark, for he knew that the fully fledged eyasses might at any time attempt their first flight, and he fervently wished to be a spectator at the event. He also knew that now was the time when the young peregrines were most vulnerable, most likely to be stolen by falconers.

He knew nothing about Tinker Smith or his plans. All the same, he had resolved many weeks ago to keep vigil during this time, and although he had not been able to find anyone who could spare the time to help him maintain a guard, he was determined to spend as many hours on the headland as possible.

Until now the mist had afforded the peregrines better protection than any he could offer, but now the skies were clear. Stars glittered in the clean cold breeze, and already the moon was silvering the waters of the Sound. He wished he had had the foresight to bring a supply of blankets, and something warm in a flask, so that he could have spent the night on the cliffs. Instead, he decided to return to the farmhouse, snatch a few hours sleep, and be back on the cliffs by first light.

Away to the south Tinker Smith sang as he stood at the wheel of his boat, watching the dark coastline slip by as he steered by the light of the moon. He was happy to be alone with the night and the white stars, happy at the thought of the money that would be his in the morning, but happiest of all, perhaps, to be his own master. He was well known in the villages and seaports along the south coast. Some said he was half gypsy, but no one knew for sure. The police knew he was an inveterate smuggler, and they knew of his illegal dealings with protected birds and eggs, but so far they had failed to catch him. Tinker had no doubt that they would be waiting for him when he got back to port, but all he would have on board would be a few mackerel and a wad of used and dirty notes, his life savings, he would stoutly declare. So he sang at the wheel, the short night passed, and as the moon rode the southern sky, the white bow wave of the boat creamed endlessly on.

The clamor of gulls, roused by the rattle of an anchor chain, woke Freya, and she raised her head from its warm pillow of plumage. It was an hour before the dawn, and the moon was sinking, spreading a carpet of milky light across the sea. The boat was a dark mass against the light of the moon. There was no sound or movement, and after a few minutes of intense scrutiny Freya decided that all was well. Her head drooped again, and once more she slept.

Sounds of splashing roused her a second time. A small black shape had detached itself from the boat and was drawing near the shore. She watched uneasily as the dinghy grated on the stones of the beach and a man got out, drawing the boat higher up onto the shore. She heard the crunch of footsteps as Tinker Smith shouldered a dark burden and set off up the beach, away from the eyrie and toward a point where the crumbling cliffs gave an easy but dangerous access to the headland. Dawn was breaking. The moon had faded and the sea was stained with the first rosy rays of the sun.

The sun sent a long finger of light through the tiny window of the bedroom where Owen Thomas lay asleep. It probed the gloom, and fell upon his face. He woke, and cursing himself for having overslept, he leaped out of bed and began to dress. Precious minutes passed as he fumbled with buttons and laces; then, pausing only to grab his telescope, together with the heavy tripod he had taken to using, he ran out of the house.

The eyasses woke to the sound of dull thudding on the cliff above their heads. Their parents flew overhead, their high-pitched cries of alarm warning the youngsters that danger threatened. Aya and Wayee crouched low on the ledge, not daring to move. Chek huddled in the far corner of the eyrie, deep in the crevice with his back to the entrance, so still and immobile that he might have been one of the rocks themselves. He heard the slithering rasp of the rope as it came snaking down, and shortly after came the grate of nailed boot on rock.

Still Chek did not move. Shadow veiled the mouth of the crevice. There was the grunting gasp of tortured breathing, the shrill cries and flapping wings of his sisters, and then the shadow lifted and the eyrie was filled with dim light again. The scrabbling sound of boots against the cliff gradually faded and died. The rope was drawn up, and then there was silence.

"Stay where you are!"

Tinker Smith groaned and swore softly to himself as he saw the burly figure of the farmer approaching. Another ten seconds and he would have been away to the beach. He glanced over the low cliff and decided it was too steep and crumbling to risk a headlong dash down to the shore. Besides, it looked as though the farmer was carrying a gun, and some of these bird-watching types were just fanatical enough to use one.

"Leave those falcons where they are, and get off this island," commanded Owen as he drew near.

An ironic chuckle escaped Tinker's lips as he saw that what he thought was a gun was just a harmless tripod. He set the basket containing the eyasses on the ground and spread his hands wide. "Look," he said depreciatingly. "Silly it is to get so angry about a couple of stupid birds. There's fifty pounds for you if you just turn round and go back to bed."

The tripod swung in a scything arc and crunched against the flesh and bone of Tinker's jaw. He dropped to one knee, shaking his head in an effort to overcome the waves of pain and nausea that threatened to overwhelm him. As Owen stood over him, he reached for a stone that lay nearby. Owen stepped warily aside. The turf of the cliff-top gave way, and as his foot plunged into a rabbit hole he fell heavily and slid headfirst over the cliff. Amid a rattle of loose stones and shale he plunged downward, to land with a thud on the grass below.

Horrified, in spite of his pain, at this sudden turn of events, Tinker threw his gear down onto the beach and then climbed down, being careful to take the eyasses with him. Swiftly, he examined the inert form of the farmer. The man was still breathing. There was no sign of bleeding, and his pulse was strong and regular. He lay above the tideline, on soft grass, and the day promised to be fine. Tinker decided to leave him where he lay. After all, it was hardly his fault that the old fool had taken a tumble. Perhaps, after he had delivered the falcons, he could phone the coast guard. He loaded the dinghy and pushed off. Already his face was stiffening, and the salt wind bit hard into the wound.

In a secluded bay off the little island of Skokholm the white yacht lay at anchor. In the cabin Tinker sat drinking brandy and counting his money while the Italian crooned over his falcons. Already Aya and Wayee were hooded and jessed, and sat perched on the hawk blocks Rossetti had provided. Tinker got stiffly to his feet and pocketed the money. "A hundred and fifty pounds," he announced with satisfaction. "I thank you very much, and now I'll bid you farewell."

Rossetti seemed hardly to hear him. With a grunt Tinker

lowered himself over the side, and within minutes the fishing boat had drawn away from the yacht.

Back on the mainland the coxswain of the lifeboat station looked out across the Sound to the little farm on Ramsey. Owen Thomas must be having a lie-in this morning. There was no sign of the flag he always flew each morning from the white pole by the farmhouse. An hour later he checked again. There was still no sign of the flag, and furthermore there was no smoke from the farmhouse chimney. The cox grew increasingly anxious, and at ten o'clock he phoned the coast guard.

Later that afternoon a pleasant-looking young man waited on the quay, watching Tinker as he tied up his boat. He lit a cigarette and sauntered over as Tinker unloaded a box of mackerel. "Been fishing then, Tinker?" he queried.

"What does it look like," snapped Tinker. He was dog-tired, stiff from his climb, and his jaw throbbed and ached. He was in no mood to play word games with the police.

"Things aren't always as obvious as they seem," smiled the detective. "Like there's this old boy who fell over the cliff on Ramsey this morning."

"Nasty," murmured Tinker.

"Oh, it's not too bad," replied the detective. "He's in the hospital, and conscious, although we haven't got a statement yet. Curious, though. The local boys tell me they found a tripod, slightly bent and smeared with blood. There's some skin and hair too, I believe. They've sent it to the forensic department for testing."

Tinker stared dully at the quay and chewed at a piece of loose skin that hung from his barked knuckles. He wondered how much the detective knew, and how much was inspired guesswork. Either way, he knew that there would be no rest for him for a while, only waiting, and the long searching questioning that might or might not lead to the truth. Either way, the future looked dark.

The policeman took him by the arm. "Come on, Tinker," he said, almost kindly, "let's go to the hospital and get that face fixed. Then we'll have a little chat."

11

First Flight

Chek sat on the ledge outside the eyrie, full-gorged and drowsy. The weather had turned chill and gray, and a cold breeze whipped the waters of the Atlantic so that the waves seethed and hissed at the base of the cliff. Four days had passed since the plundering of the eyrie, and already Chek had forgotten his sisters. He now received the undivided attention of both his parents. As a result he was suffering from a surfeit of food, for the peregrines could not adapt themselves to the reduced demands on their housekeeping and still hunted as assiduously as before. Beside Chek lay the dried remains of a rabbit, the hind legs still intact inside the furry pelt. Blowflies buzzed around the corpse of a rock dove, fresh killed that morning and untouched save for a few slivers of flesh carved from the breast. Chek hiccoughed violently and brought up a pale gray casting of feather and bone. It plopped, soft and moist, onto the ledge, and Chek eyed it, head on one side, as if its sudden appearance puzzled him.

The day wore on, and gradually Chek began to feel easier, less jaundiced, as his system adjusted itself to the sudden increase in diet. He stood upright, legs stretched, and flapped his wings vigorously. The breeze that had blown all day was strengthening, hitting the cliffs and sweeping upward in sudden gusts and drafts. Chek felt the lift of the air, his feet left the ledge, and in a sudden panic he closed his wings, alighting once more on the hard rock.

Abruptly his fear left him, to be replaced by a feeling of pleasure at the recollection of the experience. After a few minutes he tried again, but the fickle wind refused to cooperate with him, and, in spite of much energetic flapping, his feet remained firmly fixed to the ledge. Chek subsided, brooding, and then shuffled a little way along the ledge. Again he tried, this time quite unconsciously crouching first, before springing upwards and spreading his wings in flight.

For a moment it seemed he would drop back onto the ledge, but as his wings frantically fanned the air the wind caught him, pushing against his chest with the gentle pressure of a soft, uplifting hand. For a full thirty seconds he hung in the air, a foot above the ledge, before tumbling down to land asprawl among the bones and debris that littered the rock. He shook himself vigorously and automatically began to preen the long pinion feathers of his wings. Ten minutes later he was trying again, polishing and perfecting his technique, so that his performance improved with each successive launching. It was late in the afternoon before he tired and dropped his head in slumber.

An hour later he woke, refreshed and exuberant, and promptly spread his wings in fresh remembrance of his new-found amusement. Now the wind was no longer playful. It slammed upward with the force of a clenched fist, flinging Chek aloft, far above the ledge, and holding him pinned for a long moment against the overhang above the eyrie. Chek screamed, his wings stiff-spread in a wide arc over his head, as the wind released its hold and he began to fall. Then he was rising again, his wings working furiously as another gust swept him in a circle out over the sea, before hurling him back against the cliffs.

Chek saw the mouth of the eyrie loom in front of him. His wings scrabbled the air, and his feet stretched out toward sanctuary, but at the last minute he was drawn up and dropped gently on a wide, sloping shelf of rock ten feet above the eyrie, and a little to the right. There he lay, gasping and shaking, until his racing heart slowed, and the paralysis of fear left him.

He stood up and shook himself. Then, his ruffled feathers trembling in the draft, he stalked to the edge of the shelf and peered down. A gust of wind buffeted him, tip-tilting him as it caught his broad tail, and he shrank back, cowering from the force of the wind and fear of the wide gulf that lay between him and the eyrie. Pressing close to the cliff wall, he crept back along the shelf and wedged himself firmly in the corner, crouching morosely against the gray slate.

He was still hunched there when Freya flew in with a freshly killed lapwing dangling from her talons. She lighted on the ledge outside the eyrie and called. Chek answered, and Freya rose a foot above the ledge in astonishment. Then she peered upward, saw Chek on the shelf, and stared for a long time, her beak half-open, before calling again, sharply and imperiously. Chek pattered across the shelf and gave a plaintive mew, but Freya stalked into the eyrie, exploring every inch of the now deserted crevice. Only when she was fully convinced that no peregrine eyass was there did she emerge.

Chek continued to mew, his face just visible above the shelf. Freya flew up to him, the lapwing still clutched in her talons, and hovered over him. For a moment she almost alighted, only to rise again and fly back to the eyrie. Chek refused to be tempted. He was hungry, but even the thought of food would not lure him from the safety of his shelf. He marched resolutely back to his corner, remaining there while Freya plumed and dissected the corpse of the lapwing.

After Freya had eaten about half the bird, she relented, and carrying the corpse up on to the shelf, she fed Chek, urging him with sharp impatient cries to hurry and finish the meal. By now it was almost dark. Black wispy clouds ran low across the leaden sky, bringing sharp flurries of rain, and the sea crashed and thudded against the rocks with a deeper, more menacing boom.

Chek passed a wretched night, for although Freya and Frika stayed beside him on the ledge, and tried to shelter him as best they could, he was now too big to take refuge beneath their outstretched wings. Chek was as tall as Frika, although not so compact and well knit. So he crouched, a long-legged, lanky juvenile, whimpering in fear and discomfort as the wind hammered against the face of the cliff and the rain lashed across his exposed back.

Toward dawn the rain stopped and the skies began to clear. Ragged black clouds, dark riders of the night, raced across the moon, to be hurled by the wind into the shadows that lay across the sleeping land. As the sun rose, the wind dropped, and only the heavy tumult of the sea, jade green and cream under a sky of eggshell blue, remained to tell of the fury of the night.

Several times during the day Chek attempted to climb back down into the eyrie, keeping as close to the face of the cliff as he could, and moving gingerly over the sloping shelf of rock. Each time he tried, his talons began to slip and scrape on the smooth surface of the polished stone as it fell steeply away to the sea, and as he felt himself sliding into space he scrambled back, wings flapping madly. After each attempt he scurried into the corner and crouched facing the cliff wall, as if the fear of falling made him sick.

Freya came with food and circled around above the shelf, calling loudly, but although Chek was hungry, he refused to budge. Left alone again, he preened himself a little, slept a while, and woke with the afternoon sun warm on his back. He called for food, and Freya launched herself from a ledge on the cliff close by and flew past the shelf. She swooped down almost to sea level and then swept up, to light like a giant moth on a sloping green stretch of turf about a hundred yards away from where Chek sat and halfway down the cliff.

Three times she did this, each time passing so close to

Chek that he felt the rush of air as she swept by. It was an exercise in mime, a demonstration of the ease of flight, the safety of the sky, and the suitability of the green lawn of turf as a soft landing place. After Freya had sketched the plan a few times Chek got the message and followed, launching himself into the air with winnowing wings. Suddenly he felt buoyant, floating, at ease with the element, and he soared skyward, his wings stiff spread and his tail fanned out behind him. He moved a wing tip, saw earth and sky tilt as he changed direction, and hurriedly corrected the maneuver. On the cliff he saw his mother, calling shrilly from the carpet of turf, and he planed down toward her. He intended to alight beside her, but he had not yet learned how to control a landing. For a moment it seemed that he might miss the square of turf altogether and fall down into the sea, but at the last minute he fanned the air and pitched headlong onto the soft grass, close to the cliff edge.

Frika arrived with the headless body of a pigeon, which he dumped on the turf before vanishing over the headland. Freya seized the bird and was soon busily at work, making the feathers fly from its breast. Chek hurried over, and Freya thrust a portion of meat into his beak, swallowing the next mouthful herself. For a few morsels more they shared the carcass, and then Freya flew off, leaving Chek to devour the remainder of the meal. By now he was quite accustomed to feeding himself, and if he lacked the almost surgical skill with which the older birds dissected a corpse, he could still manage to tear one apart.

His flying rapidly improved, as he progressed from short cliff-to-cliff hops to soaring flights out over the beach and bay. On the second evening he climbed with his parents high into the sky, and the sunlight shone on the trio as they hung like stars above the ancient cliffs.

There was no one to watch their flight. Owen Thomas lay in a hospital ward many miles away, and the doctors, still studying his X rays, were doubting whether he would ever be able to farm again. His right leg was broken. That would heal, but in falling down the cliff he had caused massive damage to the plexus of nerves in his right shoulder. He might never move his right hand or arm again, and even if life did return to the muscles, it would be many months, or even years, before he would be able to use them properly.

After they had told him the news, he lay for a long time in silent thought. Unless he could work the farm, he could not afford the tenancy of the island. His lease was up for renewal that autumn, and he had but a short time to make up his mind. He tried to see himself attempting to fish and farm with a withered right arm, and he knew that it was better to let go, to say goodbye, rather than grow embittered with his handicap and filled with hatred for the hard, unyielding mistress he had loved so long, so well.

12

Chek the Hunter

Three falcons hung in the sky, two thousand feet above the white-capped waves. Each maintained station, wings stiff spread, tails fanned out against the moving current of air, hanging like trout in the swift cold current of a mountain stream. In absolute economy of effort, precisely, delicately balanced on the knife edge of the airstream, they remained motionless, waiting in ambush.

Far to the west, midway to the horizon, shearwaters passed in endless procession, a wavering concourse, dark wings barely skimming the waves. Here and there small groups of guillemots followed the same path, their rapidly whirring wings and direct course in strong contrast to the graceful, dipping flight pattern of the larger birds. Gannets flew higher, seemingly unhurried, yet rapidly overtaking all the other birds. It was evening, and the sea birds were returning to the islands, crops and bills laden with food for the hungry young.

To the east lay the land, its shaggy, ancient, gray-green hide cloaked in a patchwork quilt of faded gold and bronze, as the ripening crops mellowed in the summer sun. Among the lichened rocks the western gorse poured its molten gold over the spreading embers of the heather. It was as if all the wealth and suffering, all the spilt blood and lost riches of mankind, had been transmuted into the living miracle that was summer. On the mainland, cattle drifted across small squares of verdant green, their movements so slow as to be almost imperceptible, and a car like a shiny green beetle crawled along the white ribbon of road.

Save for the sea birds and the rabbits, the island lay deserted. Neighbors had come and carried off Owen Thomas's stock, and the house stood shuttered and barred. One chicken remained, stalking nervously around the deserted buildings and clucking softly to herself. She had proved too fleet of foot to catch, and at last the urgent demands of the falling tide had forced the men to abandon her. There was plenty of food for her, but she missed the companionship of the rest of the flock.

Chek saw all this, and more. He saw the buzzard low in the sky, quartering the cliffs to the south. He saw a blackbird perch on a wall before diving for cover in a blackthorn thicket, and he watched the sinuous form of an adder as it slid off the rock and took shelter for the night among the heather stems. Daily, almost hourly, he had grown in mastery of the air, so that now it had become a highway—

tangible, substantial, an intricate, shifting, changing pattern of currents and cross currents, eddies and calms, great uplifts and downchutes, pathways to be followed and used. No physical effort was required. He learned to slide down to sea level, to flatten out above the waves, riding the blast that carried him headlong, at thirty miles an hour, straight for the base of the cliffs, knowing that seconds before he crashed into the rocks the current would sweep up, climbing the cliff face and carrying him with it. He was of the wind, and by it, carried along in its embrace, yet ever free to break away, to use it just so long as it served its purpose. The thermal that took him and flung him a thousand feet into the sky lost its hold and surrendered him the moment he closed his wings, to drop earthward at a hundred miles an hour.

The slow minutes passed, and the peregrines seemed content to hang, idle and disinterested, in the evening air. Several pigeons had gone by, each noted in turn by the falcons, without attracting more than a glance. Suddenly Freya broke station, falling seaward in a wide, curving arc that carried her half a mile away from the other two. Frika and Chek watched her go, each bird alert and attentive. Already they had seen the object of her maneuver. A rock dove approached from the north east, far from land and flying into their ambush. To gain the sanctuary of the cliffs it had to pass beneath the falcons, and Freya was intent on driving it up, into the sky and into the waiting talons of her mate.

Chek had yet to make a kill. He had pounced on insects and lizards as they scurried through the grass. He had drawn the tail feathers from a moulting blackbird as it fled

screaming through the bracken, but for food he had depended entirely on the supplies brought by his parents.
Always, hitherto, he had hung back at the climax of a hunt,
in deference to the superior skill of the older birds. Now,
watching, he waited for the tiercel to take the lead.

The dove had spotted Freya. They saw it turn in sudden
panic as the falcon flew toward it in jerking, flickering
flight. Dove and falcon were climbing now, the peregrine
gaining on her prey. Frika closed his wings and stooped,
Chek following, and Freya dropped back as the tiercel
hurtled down with a whistle of air and hit the dove.
Feathers exploded in a soft gray cloud, the dove crumpled
in flight, fell fifty feet, and then righting itself flew on,
passing below Chek.

Chek did not hesitate. He saw the dove, marked its feeble
and erratic flight and closing his wings, fell toward it,
talons stretched wide. The dove heard the shrill whine of
his approach and flung itself forward in a last desperate bid
for survival. Chek saw it glance around. Every detail of
feather and pinion was clear in his eye. A split second later
he felt the satisfying thump of impact, and instinctively, as
he hit the dove, he kicked out, adding more force to the
strike. The dying dove spiraled down to the sea below, and
screaming with excitement, Chek plummeted after it, catching it just above the waves and soaring up with it in his
grasp. At five hundred feet he dropped it again and
swooped down once more, in order to repeat the thrill of
his first catch.

Frika and Freya followed sedately behind as Chek bore
his prize back to the cliff. Alighting, Chek stamped hard on
the carcass of the dove, pinning it down before he began to

plume it. As his parents hovered near he mantled his kill with brooding wings and hissed at them in warning. Freya and Frika slipped away, and ten minutes later they had killed again. Freya fed first, and then abandoned the carcass to Frika.

Chek killed several times in the days that followed, always in company with his parents. On two occasions the prey had already been hit and wounded before he made his strike, but whether this was by accident or design on the part of the older birds may never be known. The peregrines may have been teaching Chek how to hunt, or they may simply have come to regard him as a member of the team. Freya and Frika frequently failed to knock down their victims on the first strike. The doves were tough and fast, strong flyers who knew how to swerve and dodge at the crucial moment. Often, too, the falcons struck in mere sport, drawing blood and feathers from their terrified victim before allowing it to fly on unmolested. Or again they would kill and let the corpse fall unwanted into the sea, to provide food for the crabs and fish and carrion-eating gulls. The mind behind the dark proud eye and piercing glare defied all attempts to read its secrets.

As summer swelled to full ripeness, as the combine harvesters began to clatter in the fields, and the sleek gray seals foregathered on the beaches of the island, Chek learned many things. He discovered that it was a waste of time to chase the herring gulls that drifted to and fro in front of the cliffs. The gray-backed gulls simply tilted a wing tip and slipped away, avoiding his stoops as easily and as unhurriedly as if he were a lumbering buzzard.

He gave a wide berth to the fulmars. Smaller than the

herring gulls, stoically brooding their single chicks throughout the long weeks of parenthood, fasting for days at a time while their mates were away fishing at sea, the fulmars had been highly successful at colonizing the sea coasts. In less than a hundred years they had spread from the northernmost tip of the Outer Hebrides, as far south as Cornwall, and east to the Norfolk coast. Each year their colonies grew, and their numbers knew no check. Like the shearwaters and petrels, they spent much of their lives far out to sea, only returning to land for the purpose of breeding. The fulmars had a defensive weapon they did not hesitate to use, and one which Chek quickly learned to avoid, for once, when he harried a fulmar and attempted to drive it off its nesting ledge, the bird had opened its beak and ejected a dark stream of hot brown oily liquid, which spewed over his head and breast, and defied all attempts to remove it.

Bayoo the buzzard was harmless, and Chek was taught, by his parents, the sport of buzzard baiting. Bayoo ate anything—frogs and beetles, dead fish and snakes, voles and mice and nestling birds. The carcass of a sheep would keep him content for days. Best of all he liked rabbits, young and tender and fat with the feeding of summer, and he came to the island in search of these, coasting low over the turf and heather or hanging as if suspended from an invisible thread over the bracken-strewn wastes of the hills.

Frika, particularly, was loath to tolerate the presence of the buzzard over the island, and it was he who first led Chek on an attack. As Frika skimmed the heather, Chek followed, half-fearful, half-exhilarated. Bayoo rose vertically, as if hoisted on a spring, and with slow beating wings climbed in a wide circle. Frika followed, rocketing skyward at such speed that he passed Bayoo at twenty miles an hour, only to dive again and miss the buzzard by inches.

Bayoo wailed and moaned, kicking out at his tormentor, righting himself and climbing again as Freya and Chek joined in the chase. Higher and higher they climbed, Bayoo rolling on his back and kicking and snapping at the swirling wings and the outstretched talons which seemed to assault him from all directions.

A great bank of cloud loomed ahead, its apparently solid walls losing substance as they approached, until suddenly buzzard and peregrines were lost in a gray world of swirling mist and vapour. When they emerged, flying in bright sunlight above a rolling carpet of pale pink snow, Bayoo was gone. He had fallen five hundred feet and sped away into the setting sun, abandoning all hope of further rabbiting and anxious only to regain peace and solitude.

Chek soon began to hunt alone, and in earnest, and now the evening flights with his parents, the abortive attacks on the herring gulls, and his playful sporting with the buzzard, came to his aid. He killed a jackdaw as it planed in to feed in a stubble field, sending its body spinning like a scrap of burnt paper into the hedge, from where he retrieved it with some difficulty. He scooped a starling from under the nose of a surprised sparrow hawk and sped away, pursued by the angry chittering of the short-winged hunter. At last, after many unsuccessful attempts, he killed his first pigeon, stooping on it in the grand manner and stunning it, knocking it out of the sky with such force that it bounced six feet above the heather. Mortally wounded, it was just crawling away when Chek fell on it, desperately crushing its life away.

Always he returned at sunset to the cliffs of his island home, but now, like his parents, he roosted on a ledge of rock, impervious to wind and rain. The eyrie lay dusty and deserted, the bones, skin and flesh of many a meal mouldering and drying, waiting for the winds of autumn to blow them away and leave the ledge clean and bare.

13

Chek the Wanderer

Autumn came, with gales bringing gray clouds and gusty spatters of cold rain that lashed against the cliffs and flattened the dying bracken. The high tides of the equinox washed the beaches clean, shifting the decaying tangle of flotsam high onto the shores. Below the deserted eyrie the gray seals fought and loved while the calves lay fat and white and sleek among the stones.

The sea birds had gone, and the cliffs lay silent, deserted save for the drifting gulls and a solitary shag arrowing his way over the tumbling waves. An aura of change hung over land and sea, an air of unease and restlessness. The days were shortening, and the nights were full of the whisper of wings as the migrants passed, dark against the stars, each individual responding in blind obedience to the call of its kind.

Chek heard the call. At first it was small and weak, easily stilled by short flights of exploration along the coast or eastward over the heather-clad slopes of the Prescelly Hills, but daily it grew louder, more persistent, until its tone was constant and shrill, for Chek was a peregrine, a wanderer. The fusion of desire that had resulted in his conception was more, far more, than a mere brute mating, and the forces at work were beyond understanding, beyond measurement.

From his parents Chek inherited the physical characteristics that betrayed his lineage—the dark noble eye and the proud warrior's cap, the sickle-shaped wings and powerful talons. Yet this was not all, for the chromosomes that carried the keys to his physical construction brought something less tangible, less easily explained in terms of physics and chemistry. In his genetic make-up was a complete data bank of peregrine law, all the inherited wisdom of his kind, knowledge so profound and reliable that it had guided and protected his tribe through untold centuries, against an environment ever changing and often hostile. While man allowed his instincts to crumble into ruin, choosing instead to build on the shakier foundations of reason and objectivity, Chek, in abiding faith and innocence, followed his destiny, his doom—the decree, whether good or evil, of his Teutonic ancestry. By so doing, he not only survived as an individual, but helped to guarantee the future of his kind.

He flew north, skirting the coast, while below him the country unfurled its neat green pastures, sparkling streams, and dark waving tresses of woodland. He passed over lumpy hills, rising above the plains in smooth rounded

126

billows, where tiny white dots that were sheep grazed on the scanty vegetation and half-wild ponies stamped and snorted as the wind caught their manes. He saw towns for the first time and veered off course to avoid the pall of smoke and stale air that hung over them. As the setting sun stained the sky and lit the swelling, shifting columns of cloud that billowed up from the eastern horizon, he came to the high mountains of northern Wales. Here, on a granite crag, overhanging a dark waste of scree that slipped sheer down to the still waters of a lake, he slept, and for a few hours at least, the voice was still.

Dawn came, and from his lofty crag Chek looked out, over a sea of mist that lay across the valley, to the mountain peaks beyond. As the sun rose, it shone across the naked rocks, highlighting the dusky pink of the granite and softening the deep shadows of the hollows and coombes. Jackdaws were calling farther down the hill, and the sound woke hunger in Chek. He dropped off the crag and planed down through the still air, sighted the flock, and stooped. He killed, clumsily, for he was still very inexperienced, and flew back to the crag where he had passed the night.

He had broken into the kill and taken a few morsels, when he heard the high-pitched, chattering call of another peregrine. He waited and watched, listening for a repetition of the sound, before continuing to feed. Instinct told him to beware, to hurry and be gone, although he did not understand why. From time to time he paused in the act of tearing at his quarry to gaze up and around, and on the third occasion he saw the other falcon, a tiny speck high above the crag on which he perched.

The speck grew larger as the falcon dropped toward

him. Chek lingered a few moments longer, and then, satisfied that he had eaten the better part of the jackdaw, he slipped off the ledge and sped away, hugging the side of the mountain. The falcon followed, still chittering angrily, but making no real attempt to catch him. Like all juvenile peregrines, Chek ran the risk of inadvertently intruding on another peregrine's territory, and when this happened, as now, he knew better than to stop and argue. He flew fast and straight, and the falcon followed him for three miles before abandoning the chase and hanging motionless in the sky. Had he continued to trespass, or had he disputed the falcon's territorial right, she would not have hesitated to attack, and Chek would not have escaped without severe punishment. As things were, each bird had obeyed the rules, and no harm was done.

Chek flew on, and the high mountains gave way to lowland hills, and so to a flat, fertile plain. This was rich grassland—dairy country—tamed and thickly populated, the roads crowded with vehicles and the small towns busy with commerce. None saw Chek as he passed overhead, for he flew high, not pausing even to harry the vast flocks of pigeons that he saw. Ahead of him lay the industrial north, with its mills and looms and steelworks, and the cold hand of pollution held the living landscape in a grip of death. The rivers ran black and oily to the sea. No salmon forced their way upstream, and no herons fished by the water's edge. No trees grew, and on the heaps of poisoned waste the thin grasses had long since withered and died. Chek turned east, to where the hills once more hunched their shoulders against the sky, and so reached the foot of a long spine of mountains, the backbone of England, where the clean cold wind swept away the soot and stench of pollution and the heather shone purple on the dark mantle of the hills.

These were the Pennines, a massive upland of millstone grit and limestone, a desolate waste of peat bog and marsh grass and untold acres of heather, stretching as far as the eye could see. The landscape looked as old and unchanged as the ancient hills, untouched by the hand of man since time began, yet this was far from the truth, for these were grouse moors, strictly preserved and carefully maintained.

The red grouse was a bird found only in Great Britain. Slightly larger than a pigeon, it inhabited the high moors and mountains, feeding on flowers, seeds, and berries, but mainly on the young shoots of sprouting heather. The grouse was good to eat and, being a fast flyer, rising rapidly from cover and whirring rapidly over the heather, it had become a popular sporting bird with those landowners seeking something to shoot with their newly acquired shotguns.

In their natural state grouse were few in number, each bird occupying about five acres of moorland, so the landowners set about the task of increasing their stocks. Grouse needed heather, so heather was encouraged to grow. Heather needed dry conditions, so the moors were drained. The bogs, with their carpet of sphagnum moss and cotton grass, dried out, and heather grew instead.

Heather was long-lived and slow in growth, taking a quarter of a century to reach maturity, by which time it was tall and woody, standing as high as a man. As it began to degenerate and die back, the heather made way for saplings of birch and pine, and left to itself, the moor would have reverted to woodland and scrub. To prevent this happening, the moors were burned at regular intervals, and the burning was carefully controlled to ensure that at all times there was young heather to provide food for the grouse, as well as slightly older vegetation to afford shelter from the cold and safe cover for nesting.

At the same time predators were ruthlessly exterminated. Thus cosseted and protected, the grouse thrived, until each square mile of moor might hold as many as three hundred grouse. Yet in spite of everything man could do, there were years when the grouse did not prosper, when their numbers declined so drastically that the opening day of the shooting, the twelfth day of August, was a hollow mockery of what the shooters had come to call "The Glorious Twelfth."

Like all birds, the grouse carried parasites, and in their natural state the parasites caused little harm to their hosts. One of these was a threadworm, which lived on the heather and was accidentally swallowed by the grouse when the bird grazed on the young shoots. In the digestive tract of the bird the threadworm paired with another individual and laid eggs which were passed out in the droppings. In a damp summer these eggs took only a fortnight to hatch and grow to maturity, and so the grouse, living in what were to them conditions of gross overcrowding, soon fell victims to epidemics of over-infestation. They weakened and died, and so robbed the gunmen of their sport.

Long years of war, when the moors were neglected as keepers and estate workers were called away to serve in the armed forces, added to the decline. Now sheep grazed the heather instead of grouse, and so, except in a few places, the sport never regained its pre-war popularity. In the

Western Highlands of Scotland it had never enjoyed much of a vogue, for here grouse were considered a nuisance, interfering with the sport of deer stalking by flying out of the heather on the approach of the stalkers and giving noisy warning to the deer of the approach of man. Only in the Eastern Highlands, and here on the north eastern slopes of the Pennines, on the rocky ramparts between Lancashire to the west and Yorkshire to the east, did grouse shooting survive with any vestige of its early importance.

On a morning in early October, Chek rode a thermal high above the crest of a hill and looked down on a scene that might well have been the preparation for a battle. By the side of a sandy track stood a small knot of vehicles, land rovers and estate cars, and beside them waited a group of men and dogs. Over the brow of the hill, and hidden from the cars by the steeply rising ground, were a number of small, semi-circular structures built of turves, rectangular slabs of peat cut from the surrounding moor, spaced wide apart, and spread in a wide crescent along the hill, just below the crest of the ridge. The butts, as they were called, were roofless, and in each one waited a man with a gun. Behind him stood another man, the loader, and he too held a double-barreled shotgun, ready loaded, which he would hand to the man in the butts in exchange for the one just fired. The shooter could keep up a steady fire as the birds came over, for the grouse shooter did not go in search of his quarry but waited for it to be brought to him.

Already the sun was hot; blazing across at an angle, with an autumnal intensity of light and heat that faded the wine stains of dying heather blooms and made sportsman and loader alike mop his moist brow and think longingly about lunch. Meantime they waited, while far below them a long line of men and boys moved slowly toward them up the hill. These were the beaters, armed with sticks and flags, who slowly and carefully drove the grouse toward the butts. No one saw Chek, wheeling in slow circles high above the ground, and Chek, curious and unafraid, continued to watch.

The first covey of grouse burst from the heather and flew toward the butts on rapidly whirring wings, shouting their barking call. As they drew near the brow of the hill they rose into the air, passing over the heads of the shooters. Chek saw small flashes of light, heard the faint pop of the exploding cartridges, and watched as the grouse fell from the air, to bounce on the leathery, hard-baked ground and lie amid crumpled shrouds of wings.

Chek slid away to the east, into the sun and over to the right flank of the sportsmen. Then he checked and waited as a second covey of grouse began their flight toward death. He marked a hen bird in the rear of the flock and fell a thousand feet in a long shallow dive that made the air scream through his pinions. Even as he hit the bird he was climbing again, rising on rapidly beating wings and bearing his prize away before the astonished eyes of the men. The rest of the covey passed unharmed over their heads. A few drops of blood fell from the grouse and were lost in the heather. Chek was a hundred feet above the butts and fifty yards away when someone took hasty aim and fired.

The shot went wide, and the other guns were checked by a shout from the owner of the grouse moor. He stood rapt in admiration, watching the rapidly diminishing form of the peregrine vanishing with one of his birds. Never in his life had he seen anything so spectacular as the breathtaking splendor of the falcon's stoop. He knew he would dine out for many a month on the story, and if it grew in the telling, well, it would be no worse for that. As he turned back to await the next flight of grouse, he felt as lighthearted and carefree as a boy.

Chek vanished into the rock strewn wilderness of the border country, forgotten by time since the Roman Hadrian had built his great wall. Here the legionaries had waited and watched, shivering with cold, their bones aching with rheumatism from the damp and chill, dreaming of the hot sun and warm wines of their native land as they fought back the marauding bands of savage Picts and Scots.

Now they were gone, and their empire with them. Wild goats roamed across the misty fells and played among the ruins of a once mighty fort. Chek might well have lingered here, but the urge to wander was still strong within him, and he flew on, passing over the lowlands of Scotland, where great flocks of sheep grazed over gentle, grassy hills, past the spreading sprawl of the port of Glasgow, into the blue highlands, where lochs lay like pools of spilled silver in the hollows of the glens and mountains towered to the sky. On and on he traveled, north and west, until he came to the sea again. Here the coastline was tortured and split, the sea sending long fingers probing inland to where the mountains climbed three thousand feet up to the clouds. Here was the home of the deer and the wild cat, the eagle and the pine marten, a land without compromise, untamed and free. At dusk of a misty autumn day, when the waters of the sea loch lay as smooth as spread silk, Chek flew up on to the eastern face of the mountain known as An Teallach. The sun set, and as the shadows spread, the form of Chek faded and became one with the weatherworn wilderness of stone.

14

The Poison on the Land

The time of the harvest had passed, and the land lay at rest, awaiting the cold blessing of winter and the cleansing action of the frost, which would rid the ground of much of its burden of parasites and disease. The harvest had been a good one, and the farmers shared the new-found affluence that was sweeping the country after years of war and post-war austerity. Throughout those years the nation had remained well fed and healthy, but they had been starved of variety and denied material wealth. Now they were determined to sample both.

With a speed unsurpassed in the history of mankind, traditional farming methods were washed away in a tide of

136

innovation and change. The countryman plodding behind the plow learned to become a highly skilled technician, controlling thousands of pounds worth of equipment. To support him in this role a whole new industry was born. It supplied the farmer with the machines to sow and harvest his crops and the fuel with which to run them. It supplied fertilizers and foodstuffs, and it provided a network of transport to take away the produce and distribute it among the towns.

Yields continued to grow to meet the ever-increasing demand. The only commodity that did not expand was space, and as land grew more valuable, so it became more overcrowded. Chickens, pigs, and calves were condemned to eke out their short existences in specially designed houses, constructed to ensure that each animal occupied no more room than the absolute minimum necessary for survival. To feed all this stock, grain was imported, and the seas were swept for fish to supply extra protein to the diets. Since homegrown grain was cheaper than that bought from overseas, every available acre was put to the plow.

Inevitably, under such conditions of overcrowding, pests and diseases were bound to increase, and to combat these a whole new armory of drugs and chemicals was brought onto the market. The need for such drugs was so great, and the demand so urgent, that many products came on the market without being properly tested and before anyone sufficiently realized the implications of their use.

Throughout the dry dusty days of autumn the fields echoed to the roar of the tractors as the shining plowshares carved into the earth. Then came the harrowing, as the farmers sowed the new season's crops of winter wheat and barley. For years the crops had suffered from the depredations of insect pests, and man had tried in many ways to combat the menace, partly by rotating crops, and partly by dressing the seed with various substances which, it was hoped, would make it noxious to the pests. Lately a new product had appeared on the market, an organic chemical called dieldrin, which proved remarkably effective against such age-old enemies of the farmer as wireworms, leatherjackets, and wheat-bulb flies.

Soon farmers were using the substance over hundreds of thousands of acres, from the flatlands of the Fen district, to the high uplands of Wiltshire. The seed merchants dressed the corn; the farmers planted it and then waited for the rain to come and moisten the land, so that the seed would swell and germinate. The weather remained dry. The seeds lay in the fine powdery soil, and the wind came and stripped the covering of earth from the seed, exposing it to the air and to the sharp eyes of the birds. Having found the feast, the birds flocked to it, and after picking up the exposed grains, scratched around until they discovered more. Then they began to die.

The first bird to succumb in the gusty Pembrokeshire fields was a rook, a frugal bird who had toiled diligently, year after year, helping to rid the land of the very pests against which the farmer now dressed his seed. Every spring he had walked sedately over the fallow land, probing and delving with his beak, gleaning with meticulous care every wireworm, every cockchafer grub, every leatherjacket turned up by the plow. He and his relatives between them accounted for untold thousands of insects each year, and all he asked in return was a few handfuls of grain when it would least be missed.

Before he died he fed well, for several days passed before he began to feel the first effects of the poison. Then he grew drowsy and disoriented and flew in circles for a while before falling to the ground, his head shaking and his whole body seized in the throes of violent convulsions. Before death came to ease his suffering, his heart and brain had suffered damage from hemorrhages, his kidneys were totally destroyed, and the ulcerated walls of his bowels ran blood.

Now other birds began to die, some quietly, in secret places where their passing went unnoticed, others in the open, their beaks gaping, their bodies twisting and jerking, their heads shaking grotesquely as their bleary eyes gazed helplessly out on an alien world. As, slowly, man began to realize that all was not well and to cast around for some explanation for the suffering and death that lay all around, the scavengers of the wild began to play their part in the grisly performance.

Then they too began to die. Bayoo the buzzard lay spread in the heather, his head hidden beneath his outstretched wing. A vixen stumbled blindly along the cliff path, blundered into a rock, and fell mercifully to her death in the sea below. Magpies and carrion crows that had fed on the poisoned corpses of birds shared a common fate, for no bird or mammal, whatever its way of life, seemed immune.

A weasel ate two voles and a field mouse, each of which

had fed on the poisoned grain and were waiting for death. A sparrow hawk took a chaffinch and a yellowhammer, each of which was already doomed to die. She also killed and ate a skylark, which had fed on insects impregnated with dieldrin. Both weasel and sparrow hawk died, but no predator came to bring them a quick and merciful release.

The wood pigeons and the rock doves were among the first birds to suffer, for they were greedy feeders and regular visitors to the fields. Long before they died, they grew slow and lethargic, easy prey for Frika and Freya, and within a week Frika was showing the first signs of poisoning. For two days he clung to life, perched on a ledge on the mainland cliff. The world was dark, so he could not go in search of the water he craved as the fires burned inside him. Instead he crouched helplessly, the cliff face below him stained with the story of his indignity and suffering. The moon waned, the flame of his life went out, and the flesh of his body grew cold.

Rain fell at last, plumping the soil and binding it to the earth, swelling the grain so that the green sprouts sprang forth, symbols of rebirth and eternal life. Yet in successive years the poison was to claim many more victims, especially when the weather was dry, and the seed, whether spring or autumn sown, lay for long periods without germinating.

Worst hit were the predators, particularly the birds of prey, and of these the peregrine suffered most of all. From the white cliffs of Kent, along the coasts of Sussex and Hampshire to Dorset and Devon and the long rocky arm of Cornwall, jutting out into the Atlantic, investigators found the same grim story of eyries deserted and abandoned. By the early nineteen sixties the peregrine as a breeding species was virtually extinct along the south coast, and in Wales, Northern England, and Southern Scotland the situation was little better.

Frika died from dieldrin poisoning, but this was only one of a wide range of toxins newly released on the countryside as the manufacturing chemists opened a latterday Pandora's box of pesticides. In response to pressure, the government introduced a partial ban on aldrin, dieldrin, and heptachlor, but their use was still widespread, and other insecticides were used without any restrictions whatsoever.

Freya lived on. She suffered only mild ill effects from the poisons she ingested, and after a winter of wandering in the central mountains of Wales she returned to the Ramsey eyrie with a new mate, a young tiercel from Finland. Their courtship was to be in vain, for the poison in Freya's system was still exacting its toll, in some way inhibiting her calcium metabolism, so that of the three eggs she laid, one was infertile, and the other two had abnormally thin shells. These broke beneath her as she lay incubating them, and she ate the remains, not understanding, nor pausing to ask why.

The following year she tried again, and again she failed to produce the calcium needed to manufacture a sufficiently strong shell for her eggs. The eyrie joined a long list of others, once-proud haunts of peregrines since time untold, that now lay dusty and derelict or provided hovels for ravens or crows. Although by now the island of Ramsey had become a bird sanctuary, managed by the Royal Society for the Protection of Birds, and although each spring

141

the sea birds returned, to shout and jostle on the nesting ledges, the peregrines no longer hung above the clifftops, suspended from the evening sky.

The island could only provide sanctuary for the eggs and newly hatched chicks. The adult sea birds, like the peregrines, were at risk from forces outside the island. Their numbers, too, were decreasing, as birds died, smothered in the thick oil illegally discharged from tankers. Soon other sea birds were found dead, their plumage unsullied by any trace of oil, and so it was discovered that another poison was at work, this time in the sea. Over the years increasing amounts of a chemical called polychlorinated biphenyl was being produced as a waste product of the growing plastics industry. Inevitably this waste found its way to the sea, into the flesh of fish, and so to the birds. In the Irish Sea alone ten thousand sea birds died before man was even aware of the potential danger of his actions.

The island provided an ideal sanctuary for the rock doves. Unwittingly, they had exacted a terrible revenge on their age-old enemy, the peregrine, and in doing so they had paid the price of the death of many of their kind. The survivors, and they were numerous, could now breed in peace and fly with safety over the cliffs to the inland fields and pastures where they fed. The blackbird, too, sang on the fence post above the gorse thicket, and no sparrow hawk came to knock him off his perch. Fewer buzzards threatened the young rabbits that came out in the evening to feed, and new generations of voles grew to maturity without meeting the silent menace of the hunting owl.

Yet it was an uneasy peace, existing in an atmosphere of

unnatural calm, for over the living landscape hung the unanswered question, what new disaster threatened, where would it happen, and when? For one thing seemed certain, that if the death and destruction of two world wars could not put a stop to man's arrogance and greed, the death of a few thousand birds was even less likely to make him change his ways.

15

Strange Sanctuary

Daylight was dawning, and Chek stirred in sleep. From his lofty crag he looked out, over the frozen waste of driven snow and ice-clad rock. He shivered and stretched, then closed his eyes and hunched himself into a ball, ruffling his feathers against the chill. Three days had passed now since he had last fed, short intervals of light in the long tunnel of winter darkness. It had snowed almost continuously. Now he was hungry, and as the temperature fell lower and lower, he was beginning to feel the cold.

Hunger banished sleep, but still he did not stir. It was snowing again. He could feel the dry flakes tapping against his plumage. This was a strange sanctuary he had found, a harsh land where vicious gales lashed in from the sea and drove stinging showers of sleet and hail and snow against the mountainsides. Here there was little shelter, and even less food, but Chek was lean and hard and fit, and so far the weather had caused him little inconvenience. In a land where others of his kind were dying a slow and agonizing death from poison, Chek had found a corner where perhaps only the strong might survive, but which was at least free from taint and pollution.

Here in the western highlands of Scotland, where once-rich landowners had driven the peasant folk away from their homes and replaced their cattle with flocks of sheep, where sheep had given way to grouse, and grouse in turn to red deer, Chek had found sanctuary. A few years earlier, Chek would have been exterminated on sight, by men who firmly believed that any living thing that could not be hunted, fished for, or shot for sport or profit, should be destroyed as swiftly and cheaply as possible. Now those times were passing. The highlands were given over to fishing, forestry, and the stalking of red deer, and a new industry was growing, as each year more and more tourists braved the midges and the rain to discover the glories of the mountains and lochs.

The snowstorm passed, and as the light grew Chek saw that a herd of deer had moved into the basin below. Here in the hollow of the hill a wide amphitheater had been swept clear of snow by the wind, and one by one the deer dropped their heads and began to graze. The majority of the herd were hinds, but here and there the dark outline of antlers revealed the presence of a stag. As Chek watched, a hind barked a warning, and at once every head was raised, ears alert, as the herd stood poised and ready for instant flight.

At first Chek could not discern what had disturbed the hind. The intensity of his stare deepened as he watched the icy arena. Beyond the stones and the dark stretch of heather the snow lay broken and patchy, gray in the morning light. One patch moved slightly, and now Chek saw that it was a bird, its plumage as white as the snow that lay all around, one of a flock that, like the deer, was grazing on the meager covering of heather.

The ptarmigan were hardy birds, dwellers of the mountaintops, rarely coming down below two thousand feet, even in the bitterest weather. Like their cousins the red grouse, they were vegetarians, living off heather and the fruit and leaves of other mountain plants, and because so much of their lives was spent among the snowdrifts of a highland winter, their white plumage gave them excellent camouflage. In summer only their wings and underparts were white, and the rest of their plumage was mottled with brown and black. So throughout the year the ptarmigan remained an inconspicuous bird, merging with its surroundings so successfully that even Chek's sharp eye could discern them only when they moved.

A flock of ptarmigan would not disturb a herd of deer, so Chek watched and waited, knowing that there was still something that he had missed. A few seconds later another movement caught his eye, and then he saw what had alarmed the hind. A fox was moving downwind of the birds, his brush sweeping the snow as he stalked toward them. A situation was developing which Chek could well turn to his advantage, and he dropped off his perch, climbing rapidly into the icy air until he hung high above the basin.

The fox was nearer now, a mere few yards from the nearest bird, his jaws agape, white teeth bared in a mirthless grin as he crouched belly down in the snow. Any moment now he would spring, and the ptarmigan would take flight in sudden panic, whirl rapidly over the ground, and vanish behind the nearest tumble of rock. Chek began to drop, and even as his wings closed and he hurtled groundward, the fox made his pounce.

It was all over in seconds. The fox sprang. Ptarmigan exploded like giant snowflakes in a flurry of white wings as Chek passed within a foot of the fox's head. The whistle of the falcon's approach, the snap of jaws, the solid thump as Chek hit his bird, all welded and merged into one, followed by the thunder of hooves as the deer left the basin. A few dark drops of blood grew like crimson blossoms in the snow, and then there was only the wind, keening through the dried stems of heather as it passed over the empty land.

As Chek flew back to his ledge, carrying his kill tight-clenched in his talons, he saw the fox trotting downhill, tail and head held high, muzzle shrouded by white wings. Then he forgot the fox as his beak tore into the breast of the ptarmigan, and he knew once again the fierce joy of the raptor that has killed.

Not all kills were as easy, or as spectacular, for Chek was

still a juvenile, still somewhat lanky and loose knit. He lacked the split-second timing and superb judgment of the mature falcon, and so he was still prone to slight miscalculations, fractional errors that cost him a meal. When, as often happened, he fell slightly short in a stoop, his clutching talons, instead of severing the head from the body of his prey, merely kicked a cloud of feathers from the unfortunate bird's rump, giving his victim that last ounce of impetus needed to escape capture.

The majority of his victims were either very young, very old, sick, lame, or simply careless. Each signed its own doom, and in dying, admitted its failure and ceded its right to reproduce others of its kind. So Chek, like countless others of his forebears, ensured the health and vigor of other species by weeding out the weaker members of the breed.

A few days later, Chek launched himself in pursuit of a grouse. The land still lay in the grip of the frost, but the skies had cleared, and the light of the sun was reflected with harsh brilliance from the glaring white of the snow, while the shadows of the rocks and snowdrifts were deepest indigo.

The grouse flew low over the hill, one moment dark in outline against the snow, then lost and hidden by the feathery tops of heather. Chek came out of the sun, fast and steep, and hit the grouse with such force that both birds plunged deep into a snowdrift.

The snow had piled against the heather, forming a hollow cavern. Caught inside, Chek was baffled and blinded, the grouse grimly determined to fight for his life. He was an old bird, victor of many a battle fought each spring as he contested his territorial rights with other cock grouse, and he was armed with a powerful set of claws and spurs.

The impact of landing had loosened Chek's grip, and now, as he strove to blink his eyes clear of snow, to orient himself and renew his attack, the grouse leaped at him, kicking and pummeling him back into the snow. Half suffocated, smothered by the blanket of soft whiteness that enveloped him, Chek struggled to be free and burst in a miniature snowstorm out into the brightness of the world above.

The grouse was gone, lost in the maze of tunnels that lay beneath the snow-shrouded heather. Wet, bedraggled, and aching from a dozen bruises, Chek flew away, to spend a long hour drying his ruffled feathers and meticulously preening each ragged quill. As the sun began to sink he flew down to the salt marshes that lay at the head of the sea loch. There he killed a dunlin, one of a great flock that drifted like a smoke cloud over the edge of the shore, cutting it out from the flock in fine style and driving it a hundred feet into the sky before rolling over and snatching it out of the air.

Throughout the winter, the salt marsh was a favorite hunting ground for Chek. Indeed, without its existence, it is doubtful whether he would have survived the long lean weeks, for prey was scarce on the high hills. Always, the marsh was alive with movement, as flocks of birds scoured the mudflats and runnels or grazed the sea-washed turf.

Dunlin and knot and bar-tailed godwit pattered and piped and probed the shallow waters in search of small marine life. Teal and widgeon, wintering flocks of golden-eye and tufted duck, were joined by curlew, sailing in on massive, widespread wings. On the waters of the loch were mallard and eider duck, sheldrake and merganser. Always a heron fished patiently by the shore, and from time to time a solitary great northern diver came in from the sea, hugging the cliffs and rowing stealthily toward the shore, like a marauding Viking longship.

Here on the salt marsh Chek practiced his hunting skills, skimming low over the land and cutting out an individual from the flocks of waders that burst into panic-stricken flight at his approach. Often he missed, bemused and bewildered by a forest of flapping wings as the birds banded tightly together and refused to break ranks. Often he killed messily, striking again and again, as his prey, mortally wounded but desperate to escape, evaded his kicking claws. With each kill he gained experience, speed, and confidence, and frequently he would harry the flocks without shedding blood, testing his skill and speed and matching them against his prey.

The cock grouse that had given him such a beating lived for only three days after their encounter. The blow he had received when Chek hit him had left his back stiff and sore, and he stayed hidden in the snow tunnels under the heather, resting and waiting until his wounds healed. On the third evening he was scented by a hunting wild cat as she padded soft-footed over the snow. She pounced blind in the direction of the scent, sweeping away the snow with powerful forepaws. The startled grouse broke from cover and flew straight into her jaws. She hit him once, her paw catching him across the side of the head, and he was already dying as her teeth sank into his throat.

16

Chek the Homeless

The wind blew from the south, bringing warm rain. Through breaks in the cloud the sun shone, melting the snows so that the streams ran white and foaming down the mountainsides. Blackbirds sang in the birch thickets, and the rolling call of the curlew echoed over the windswept moors. After long months of imprisonment, bound in chains of darkness and ice, spring had broken free. Her legions massed in the valleys and surged out up the steeply sloping hills, and everywhere their feet touched they left a mist of green. In bygone days a chieftain who had been wronged by a neighboring clan could get from his king a commission of fire and sword against his foe. So now spring marched against the forces of winter, slaying the forces of the frost and firing every living thing with the urge to grow and reproduce.

Among the first to feel the fire of spring were the ravens, and long before the snows had left the high peaks the great black birds were aflame with desire. Each day they flew high above the tumbled masses of rock and scree, rolling and diving in their courtship dance, their acrobatics improving as their elation grew, until at times they flew upside down. Back on the ground, their courtship continued, as the male paraded in front of his lifelong mate, bowing and neck-stretching, and ruffling his throat feathers.

The ravens were carrion eaters, and they had fared well through the winter, feeding on the remains of sheep and deer that had died. These feasts the ravens shared with hooded crows, buzzards, eagles, and the lean yellow foxes of the hill, and there was never any shortage of meat. Sheep died of cold and exposure to the bitter winds. Ewes, heavy with lamb, their fleeces saturated and weighted down with wet snow, fell over and found they could not rise. Sheep and deer starved, until their frail bodies could no longer generate enough heat to combat the frost. Disease and sickness took their toll. Occasionally a hind was shot, and in her last stumbling run fell over a cliff or into some gulley from which her body could not be recovered. At all times, any animal caught by night, or in a sudden storm away from shelter, stood small chance of surviving.

No death went unnoticed by the undertakers of the hills. They waited in the skies, and their eyes were everywhere, often reading the signs of portending disaster long before death came to claim his latest victim. Then they gathered in solemn conclave, patient, enduring, sure of their reward.

Occasionally they could not wait for death, and the ravens in particular were not above pecking the eyes from a living lamb. So they were not loved by the hill farmers, and many a sitting bird was shot on her nest of eggs, although they were protected by law. Yet it was always the weak, the helpless, and the ailing that the ravens took, and a healthy lamb, mothered by a strong ewe, had little to fear. The ailing lambs would die anyway, and it was bad husbandry that killed them. The beaks of the ravens were merely the instruments of death.

Chek was not aware that the crag on the mountain where he had passed the winter was the age-old nesting site of the ravens. The previous year's nest, a solid affair of heather stems, sheep's wool, moss, and mud, had been broken down by the trampling and jostling of the young ravens before they flew off into the world. The gales and rain of winter had cleared the debris off the ledge, and now little evidence remained to indicate the whereabouts of the site.

But the ravens remembered, and one morning in April the hen bird flew up on to the ledge, closely followed by her consort. Chek, dozing in the caressing warmth of the sun, woke to hear the beating of wings and raised his head in query. At first he felt no alarm, for the ravens were a familiar sight in the skies above the mountains, and although he was dwarfed by their size, their ponderous, seemingly slow flight, and ground-feeding habits had given him little cause for fear.

Normally the ravens held a healthy respect for the peregrines, and prudently kept their distance, especially from the larger falcons. Chek was a tiercel, and moreover he was alone. The ravens attacked, the hen bird, in the lead, knocking Chek off his perch with a powerful kick of her scaly black claws.

Chek had no cause to stay and fight. Without a mate, he had no strong sense of territory, and no real desire to dispute ownership of the ledge with the ravens. He dropped down toward the valley, only to find the female hard on his heels, striving to climb above him and strike him again. He peeled off at a tangent, and began to climb, flying at a rate which left the raven far in the rear. Then he saw the male, cutting through the sky in an endeavor to head him off and turn him back to the female.

Chek shot vertically into the sky and began to climb, a thousand feet, two thousand, three, while below him the ravens followed, gaining height with remarkable speed. Seven thousand feet above the shimmering waters of the loch the ravens closed with him, and Chek found he could not get past their guard and escape in the sanctuary of a dive. Battered and buffeted by black wings, kicked and clawed, Chek was now in serious trouble. Desperately he twisted and turned, striking out at the heads of his opponents in an endeavor to stave off a lethal blow from their stabbing beaks.

Dimly he was aware that the skies were growing dark, but only when he was assailed by the sharp sting of hail did he realized that a squall had blown in from the sea, and that now he was fighting for his life in the dense clinging vapor of a storm cloud. Then lightning split the sky, and as the thunderclap broke, the three birds were flung apart, spun hundreds of feet in the tumult of the elements. Then Chek was falling, spiraling down toward the sea, only to be caught and swept inland by the gust of wind that accompanied the squall. As his senses returned he saw the rock-strewn hillside rushing below him, and wearily he spread his wings in an effort to break his fall.

Dazed, exhausted, but otherwise unharmed, he pitched down into the heather and crawled into a crevice between two rocks. There he rested, and after a while he slept.

In the late afternoon he woke and flew up onto the rocks. Immediately he began to preen himself, and the gentle exercise of stretching and bending soon eased his stiffening muscles, so that by the time his plumage was as immaculate as he wished, he felt fresh and invigorated. His adventure had carried him a long way inland, but now, climbing into the sky, he saw the glimmer of the coast in the distance. He flew toward it, reading the terrain below like a map.

Ahead lay the familiar outline of the mountain which had been his home for the winter, but even at this distance he could see the dark outline of the ravens as they perched on the ledge, brooding over the events of the day. Their presence reminded Chek of the hazards of the morning, and he veered north, crossing the narrow waters of the loch and heading for the high peaks that stood sentinel against the sea, their heads veiled in cloud.

At the foot of the mountains lay a wide valley, or strath, where a river meandered over a flat plain of peat bog and marsh. Lapwing had gathered here for their evening feed, and Chek cut one out from the flock, carrying it dangling from one foot as he flew toward the mountains. On a ledge a thousand feet up the mountainside, and overlooking the sea, he broke into the lapwing and fed. Full-gorged, he slept, as the moon climbed over the horizon and lit the slumbering hills with soft radiance. Once the night echoed to the wheezing, rasping wail of lapwings, but no ghosts came to haunt Chek's dreams. A fox had crossed the marshland where the lapwings roosted, waking them to fill the air with frightened cries.

The mountains formed a rough semi-circle, encompassing a vast arena of birch forest and marsh, interspersed with clear, rocky streams and dotted with tiny lochans. Beyond lay the shore, where sand dunes spiked with marram grass grew from the white, sea-scoured strand. Here Chek was disposed to linger. The hunting was good, and it seemed unlikely that he would be disturbed.

A ring ousel, conspicuous in his black livery and white collar, piped his song on a rock high upon the mountainside, and Chek swooped on him. The ring ousel fled, and Chek lost him in a massive assemblage of pine and birch branches, piled on a rocky crag. As he flew away Chek heard the angry rattle of the ring ousel as it scolded him from the safety of its hideout. A month ago the ring ousel had arrived from Africa, found a mate, and set up home in the base of the old eagle's nest.

A week later the eagles returned and began to repair the upper part of the nest, bringing fresh branches, some green with leaves, to add to the vast collection already assembled. Like the ravens, the eagles paired for life, and this pair had three eyries, which they used in rotation, one each year. They ignored the ousels nesting in the lower regions of the nest, and the ousels, for their part, seemed to have no fear of the great birds, with their hooked bills, massive talons, and seven-foot wingspans.

The eagles were hunters, preying on grouse and ptarmigan, swooping down on the mountain hare that was foolish enough to stray too far from cover. They also took lambs, and deer calves, and for this habit they were not loved. Many eagles were shot and their eyries destroyed, and as a result their numbers declined.

Their taste for carrion also caused their numbers to be reduced, and in many places where eagles were once common, the species was extinct. Each summer the sheep suffered severely from fly strike, as blow flies laid their eggs on wounds and the hatching maggots burrowed into the living flesh. To combat this the sheep were dipped regularly, and of late a pesticide called aldrin had been introduced into the dip. If, in spite of the treatment, some sheep then died, birds feeding on the carcasses were poisoned. Once again many birds had to die before aldrin was banned.

This pair had survived, to return to their old nesting site, and it was not long before they began to harry Chek. Their attacks were neither as concerted nor as vicious as that of the ravens, but after a week Chek's nerves began to fray under the strain. Their great size, as they swooped down from the skies at speeds of up to ninety miles an hour, made even Chek's heart race with fear, and several times he had to abandon a fresh kill, only to see it borne away in the talons of the robber giant. The last sound he heard, as he flew away from his tormentors, was the harsh scolding of the ring ousel, safe in the dungeons of the castle of sticks.

During the weeks that followed there was no peace for Chek. A pair of hen harriers pursued him down a mountainside. A short-eared owl rose from her nest on the

heather, calling to her mate. Together the two birds drove Chek from their territory and for more than an hour flew back and forth over their domain, uttering low, booming cries.

From time to time Chek strayed into territory occupied by other peregrines, and here he was least welcome of all. Time and again he fled yelping from the concerted attack of a breeding pair and learned to keep a wary eye open for the twin stars high in the sky that heralded certain assault if he did not depart swiftly.

He strayed east, over the mainland of Scotland, across barren mountains, where the only sign of life was the occasional flock of sheep or herd of deer, over dense forests of conifers and wide straths where green oats grew in a patchwork of tiny fields. The craggy peaks gave way to heather-clad moorland, falling away in gently rounded slopes, and beyond lay the glimmer of the sea.

17

The Foster Parent

A broad river flowed through parkland to the sea. In the park stood a large house, set back among the trees, and its many windows looked out across the valley and the river to the grouse moors beyond. The owner of the house was also laird of the estate, but since he was seldom in residence, the management of the estate was left to a manager—the factor—whose word was law.

The land in the valley was fertile, and the small farms were kept tidy, their buildings neat and in good repair; but farming was reckoned of little importance here, and the fields and hedgerows, the small copses that littered the hills, were all part of a landscape patterned to form one vast game preserve . Pheasants stalked through the growing corn, and partridge called from the hay fields. Salmon forged their way up the cold clear waters of the river, and on the hills the grouse made their nests in the heather.

To preserve the game a small army of keepers was employed, and they lived in a row of cottages just beyond the park gates. There were bailiffs to patrol the river, to protect the salmon from poachers and act as guides when guests of the laird came to fish. There were keepers to tend to the partridge and rear fresh broods of pheasant chicks to replace those shot in the autumn. There were keepers on the hill to manage the herds of deer and preserve the grouse moors.

In the garden of the head keeper's cottage was a wooden shed, and at the back of the shed, nailed to the rough planking, hung the corpses of those predators classed as vermin by the keepers, shot so that the game birds might survive long enough to be killed by the laird and his guests. Of all the victims, hooded crows were by far the most numerous, but they shared the gibbet with owls and sparrow hawks, buzzards and ravens. Here and there hung a dainty merlin, and even a mousing kestrel. Goosander and merganser hung head down, their death the price they paid for fishing in the laird's river.

Birds were not the only victims. Here were stoat and weasel, and the skinned corpses of otter, marten, wild cat, badger, and fox. Some of the corpses were fresh, but many had hung so long that their bodies had returned to the elements from which they came, and only their sightless skulls remained. One corpse was so fresh that the bloodstains had barely darkened on his breast. It was the body of a peregrine, shot that morning.

Earlier in the year he had flown down from the far north with his mate, and in the evenings, as the white snowdrifts gave way to the green of young heather, he had flown in courtship high above the moors. Although snow showers were still frequent, and the night air crackled with frost, the grouse were already nesting, and so the peregrines lingered, assured of an easy supply of food.

On an outcrop of rock, high in the remotest part of the moor, the falcon scraped her eyrie, and here she laid four brown-speckled eggs. By the time they hatched, the moor was alive with young grouse, feebly flying over the heather, and so the eyasses fed well. The ground around the eyrie was littered with remains of grouse, young and old, for the peregrines killed little else.

For many weeks the existence of the peregrines went unnoticed, for though the eyrie was easy of access, the moors covered many miles of hill. Now, as the weather improved, and the treacherous peat bogs dried out, the keepers ventured farther afield, sometimes on horseback, but more often on foot, a shotgun under one arm.

So the tiercel died, his life blown out by a charge of shot as he flew up from the heather with a fledgling grouse clenched in his talons. The keeper stuffed his corpse, together with the body of the grouse, into a pocket, and later he showed the tiercel to the head keeper. Both men nodded in slow agreement as they examined the body of the peregrine. Somewhere, no doubt, there was on the moor a falcon with young, and the sooner she was found, the better it would be for the grouse.

Ten miles away, the falcon waited by the eyrie, watching for the tiercel's return. Slowly the hours passed and the sun climbed higher in the cloudless sky, but no dark speck showed in the firmament of blue. The eyasses were hungry and fractious in the heat. Flies tormented them, and they yelped incessantly as they jostled and fought in the hollow of the heather.

In the late afternoon the falcon flew up and circled the eyrie, calling to her mate. She continued to call, her cries growing more urgent and appealing as the long evening drew to its close and pale stars glittered in the sky. Only when it was quite dark did she fall silent, fly down to the eyrie, and gather her hungry youngsters under her wings, brooding them against the cold of the night.

Chek heard her calls as he perched on a rock, his breast stained vermilion by the dying rays of the sun. The sound stirred him to unease, arousing emotions he did not understand, strange sensations he had never experienced before. He listened again, straining to hear, and in a way longing, yearning, for a repetition of the sound. There was nothing, only the wind in the heather and far away the distant bleat of a lamb.

He slept fitfully, and several times in the night he woke, tensed and listening. In those waking moments he was aware of some strange power at work, attracting him, luring him. By daybreak, however, the spell had broken, and in the dawn light he flew low over the moor, with hunger his only motivating force and grouse his sole objective. A small covey broke to his left and he swerved in pursuit, picking off a bird in the rear and hitting it hard. On the third strike it fell to the ground and lay kicking among the heather. Chek fell on it, wings spread wide so that he should not be overbalanced in the struggle. Seizing the head of the grouse in his beak, he crushed its brain and decapitated it with one deft twist.

Then he heard the call again, the summons seeming more urgent, more pleading than on the night before. Chek sat with head held high, gazing round as the red blood flowed from the grouse he held in his claws. He hesitated a moment more, then snatching up his prey, he flew off across the moors. A few minutes later he was circling the eyrie, and the falcon was flying below him, her cries now soft and tremulous in greeting.

Chek pitched the body of the grouse on the ground near the eyrie before landing to watch as the falcon tore the bird apart, bolting a few mouthfuls herself before stuffing great chunks of meat down the maws of the hungry eyasses. He lingered only a few minutes, and then flew off, to return in fifteen minutes with another grouse. Soon the eyasses were sated and content, collapsing in a sleepy huddle of white down. The falcon ate the remains of the grouse, and only then did Chek remember his own hunger.

So Chek became foster father to a brood of four, and consort to the bereaved falcon. In the evenings the falcon and he flew together high in the sky above the eyrie, and while these flights served a purpose, in that they established the peregrines' claim to their territory, and though often they would end in a hunting expedition, the peregrines also flew for the joy of living and the pleasure of each other's company. Between them was cemented a bond of friendship, and though in their case it was a union purely of spirit, it was a tie nothing could now part. Like all falcons, they were united until death.

Death came in the morning, a fortnight later. Ever since

killing the tiercel the keepers had been searching the moors for the eyrie they knew must exist somewhere, but although the area under their charge was relatively small, there was still over a hundred square miles of heather-clad hill to cover. As the days went by the search narrowed, as one by one the most likely sites were checked and found deserted. The keepers knew better than to waste time searching the coombes and valleys, and so made straight for the high spots, scanning every bluff and outcrop of rock with their binoculars.

At last there came a day when the falcon watched with growing unease the figures of two keepers, a man and a boy, toiling slowly up the steep and slippery side of the hill toward the low promontory where the eyrie lay. Chek was missing, hunting far away on the other side of the moor, and the falcon was alone with her young. An hour passed, and steadily the keepers drew nearer.

Not until the men were within yards of the eyrie did the falcon leave her post. Even then she did not fly far, but circled around screaming hatred and anger. The older man watched, his shotgun ready, as the boy trampled the eyasses underfoot, stamping out their lives with his nailed boots. Then, as the falcon swooped low over their heads, he fired twice, and at his second shot the falcon fell into the heather.

The boy ran over and picked her up. She was not quite dead, and her last act was to sink her talons deep into the boy's hand. Even in death she did not relax her hold, and in the end the older man had to sever her toes with his knife and draw the claws out one at a time. By nightfall the boy's hand was swollen, and deep in the wounds, pockets of

166

infection festered and grew. It was many weeks before he used his hand again.

The keepers had gone, taking the body of the falcon with them, by the time Chek returned to the eyrie. He stood for a long time, the plucked corpse of a grouse in his talons, and looked at the blood-stained corpses of the eyasses. Not comprehending, he called, sharply, but they did not move. He left the grouse and flew up into the air, circling around and calling for the falcon, but there was no answer. All that day he waited by the eyrie, calling and waiting, listening for a reply. There was nothing, only the soft sigh of the wind as it combed the heather, and the excited buzz of blow flies as they explored the remains of the eyasses.

His vigil ended with the dusk. In the afterglow of the setting sun his gray form flickered ghostlike over the darkening hills and was lost in the shades of night.

18

The Nylon Snare

Slowly, the long summer slipped away. Blackberries shone in dark clusters by the yellow stubble fields, and in the woods the smell of the soil was acrid and dank, as strange fungi thrust their way up through the decaying leaf mold. The morning mists hung about the hedgerows, silvering the spiders' webs and polishing the rose hips until they shone red in the soft autumn light. Beside the shrunken rivers the wild balsam bloomed, and bees buzzed among the pungent flowers, their bodies white with pollen. Each evening the robin sang his territorial song, and the night air was filled with the soft quavering of owls, as together they agreed on their winter hunting grounds.

Winter came early. Icy winds swept in from the north and east, bringing great flocks of migrant birds from the forests and fields of the frozen continent. The night skies were loud with the clamor of their passing—waxwings and redwings, fieldfares, starlings and lapwings. They sought wide pastures free from frost and snow, and shelter from the bitter winds of night. As the grip of winter spread, the birds drifted south and west, driven on by the wolflike howling of the wind.

Chek followed, roaming the skies and harrying the flocks of winter migrants whenever he came upon them. He was impervious to the cold and unheeding of the icy gales that brought blinding blizzards of snow. At night he roosted wherever he could find shelter, in a ruined building or broken-down wall, on a rock ledge, or high in some leafless tree. All the while he journeyed south, passing down the mountainous central spine of Wales, until at last he came to the sea.

The wind blew from the land, and dark clouds, heralds of yet another snowstorm, massed on the northern horizon. Seaward the skies were clear, and on the distant horizon the blue outline of cliffs divided sea from sky. The cliffs were the ramparts of a wild, hilly land, where red deer roamed and black grouse called from the heather.

Chek flew low over the waves, passing rafts of sea birds, puffin and guillemot, riding out the winter far from land. Some twelve miles before he reached the mainland he came to an island, a flat buttress of rock rising sheer out of the water to tower five hundred feet above the waves. A herd of wild goats grazed along the sides of the precipitous cliffs, and a gray seal rolled at the mouth of a cave. Rock doves flew up from the rocks at Chek's approach, and he dived in pursuit.

Full fed, he passed the short winter afternoon preening and dozing on a ledge sheltered from the cold bite of the wind and lit by the sinking sun. With the coming of dusk he slipped off his perch and flew along the side of the cliffs, looking for shelter for the night. A crevice loomed darkly ahead, and Chek alighted on the ledge in front of the opening, shaking himself and gazing all around him before cautiously entering the hole.

He was not alone. A peregrine lay on guard at the entrance, a peregrine long dead, whose sightless eyes stared out over the sea, as they had done night and day for over a year. Even here, on this remote island, once the hideout of pirates and smugglers, the poison spread upon the land had claimed a victim.

Chek did not linger. He left the falcon undisturbed in her rocky tomb and flew on. As night fell and the stars went out as the first flakes of snow began to fall, he came to roost in a small cave. Two rock doves flew out on his arrival, preferring to face the night, and the uncertainties of fate, rather than share their bed chamber with their arch enemy.

Snow did not lie long on the island. By morning it had begun to melt, gray against the dull green of the turf. The sea was calm, and the island was dank and cold under a shroud of mist. Chek climbed above the cloud into bright sunshine and looked out, over the rolling bank of vapor, to the mainland of Devon.

Snow lay thick and white on the high moors, but the

coastline was clear. Chek quartered the high cliffs, chased a wood pigeon into a thickly wooded coombe, crossed a broad white stretch of sandy beach, and so came to the estuary.

The estuary was broad and wide and reached far inland from the sea. Each time the rain fell, the river rose in flood, and the rushing waters brought with them thousands of tons of silt, soil washed off the fields, the very cream of Devon's rich farmland. This was deposited in the estuary, and at low tide the mud banks so formed became a rich feeding ground for hosts of waders. Once again Chek had found a winter larder, and in the weeks that followed he hunted the estuary every day. No one saw him, for to most humans the estuary was a wild and desolate place in winter. There were no houses, and Chek was careful to avoid the occasional wild-fowler, who waited, gun in hand, by the shore. The remains of Chek's kills littered the ground until they were broken up by the gulls, but no one examined them or looked for the telltale notches on the breastbone, the marks of a peregrine's hooked beak.

The winter dragged on in remorseless cold. On the inland pastures redwings died, their instincts betrayed by the snow. The river ran low as the frost gripped the moisture in the land. A kingfisher lay in the snow, his azure wings folded as if in prayer, and a hunting fox paused to sniff the corpse before continuing on his way, leaving the body untouched. There was no meat there, only a mouthful of frozen bone and feathers. As the frost bit into the land, even the sea began to freeze and ice floes drifted in the estuary as the tide rose and fell. At night the stars glittered like great frost diamonds, and their images shone in the sparkling snow.

On a gray morning toward the end of January, Chek skimmed low over the frost-rimed turf of the saltings that bordered the estuary. A flock of lapwings rose in a flurry of fear, and Chek was about to launch himself in pursuit when his eye caught a flicker of movement on the shore. Above the waves, on the high-tide mark, a sandpiper fluttered and danced, leaping a foot into the air before falling back and scrabbling on the shingle.

Chek dropped on the sandpiper, and it died in his grasp. He broke into it at once and began to feed, not bothering to carry the corpse away. Several times during the meal he stamped in annoyance, hampered by fine coils of a springy, slippery material that persisted in wrapping itself round his shanks. The more he tried to shake them off, the more his legs became entwined. At last, exasperated, he tried to fly away.

He was trapped. He rose into the air, and was pulled up short, held by the coils. He fell back on the stones and began to worry at his bonds, snipping at them with his beak. Had he worked systematically and methodically, he might well have gotten free, but each time he cut a strand, another enmeshed him.

The previous summer, an angler fishing from a boat had got his line in a tangle. Impatient and angry, he had cut away the snarled length of nylon and thrown it overboard, and the line had drifted away on the tide. The monofilament was fine but strong, able to withstand the strain of a twenty-pound weight before breaking. It had drifted ashore in the estuary, anchoring itself firmly to the masses of dried weed that lay along the high water line. It had snared the sandpiper, and now it had trapped Chek.

The hours passed, and Chek gave up struggling and slept. The nylon caused him no pain, but already it was tightening on one toe and beginning to cut off the circulation. With the coming of dusk he woke and tried again to break free, but night came, and the dawn, and Chek was still a prisoner.

The days passed, and hourly Chek grew weaker. He lost weight as his metabolism strove to keep the fires of life alight against the cold. He was visited several times and menaced by ravens and black-backed gulls, but even the boldest quailed when confronted by that indomitable glare and fierce, snapping beak.

As he lay, half-dozing, half-frozen by the cold, he was roused by the crunch of footsteps on the shingle. A man was coming, and fear of his presence woke Chek to make one last effort to escape. The feeble flapping of his wings attracted the attention of the man. He made his way over to Chek and stood for a few moments, staring at the exhausted peregrine.

He was an old man, a retired doctor, and an ardent wildfowler. He lived in the small town at the head of the estuary and spent many hours during the season waiting with his gun for the chance of a shot at duck or goose. He was also a conservationist and a member of an association that believed in preserving the birds that offered them their sport. Throughout the winter members of the association had refrained from shooting, instead providing supplies of grain to birds hard hit by the weather.

The old man carried a sack of grain on his back, and now he emptied it on the marsh, scattering it over the turf where the birds would find it. Then he returned to Chek.

Taking out his knife, he cut the tiercel free but left his legs still entangled. Then he wrapped Chek in the sack, and set off on the long trudge, back along the estuary to the town. Chek lay limp and inert in the folds of the sack, too weak even to feel fear, and gradually he slipped into unconsciousness again.

He was aware briefly of light and warmth and gentle hands cutting away the nylon line that had bound his legs and feet. Then once more he was alone in the dark and stuffy confines of a wooden box.

The old man took his gun out of its rack, stuffed a handful of cartridges in his pocket, and left the house. In an hour he was back, a brace of wood pigeons dangling from his left hand. He hung one in the larder and laid the other on the kitchen table. He split the bird open and took from it the heart and liver. Then he cut thin slices of warm flesh from the breast, and after wiping his hands, took Chek from the box.

Chek offered no resistance as the old man gently forced open his beak and pushed the food down into his crop. Reluctant to overfeed him, the old man contented himself with getting a few morsels of meat into Chek before putting him back in his box and setting him near the warmth of the stove.

Two hours later he prepared a second feed, and when he opened the box Chek was on his feet, and his eyes were open. Each successive feed grew more of a struggle, and by the time twenty-four hours had passed and the pigeon had been demolished, the old man was ruefully wishing that he possessed a strong pair of gloves.

By the end of the second day Chek was strong enough to be moved to the outhouse the old man had prepared, and he crouched in the semi-darkness, his talons gripping the rough perch, ignoring the pigeon the old man had left for him. He was left alone until the following morning, when the pigeon was removed, and a fresh one left in its place.

The pigeon was newly killed, and the old man had split it open so that its flesh steamed in the cold air. Chek regarded it with a cold stare but made no move toward it. Outside the door the old man watched through a crack in the planking, waiting as the slow minutes passed.

Chek sat as though carved from stone. Then suddenly he stretched to his full height and raised his wings above his head. Subsiding, he extended one wing and leg, scratched his poll, and shaking himself, ruffled his feathers all around him. Only then, as though he had completed a list of important tasks, did he sidle over to the pigeon. Delicately, he drew it toward him with the tip of his beak, glared all around, and began to feed.

Within a week he had regained all his lost weight. His feet were frost-bitten and took longer to heal, but soon they were on the mend, all save one toe on his left foot, where the nylon had bitten deep. This toe eventually withered and dropped off.

The weather was changing. Chek could sense it, even in the confines of his prison. Out in the Atlantic a depression was forming, deepening and intensifying as it gathered strength. The thaw, when it came, was as sudden as it was dramatic. One moment the air was still, the ground deep in the grip of the frost. Then suddenly there was a soft warmth in the air, a breeze that grew until it was a roaring gale. Snow fell, and turned to rain, and the rivers thundered down to the sea.

On a morning soft with the promise of spring, as a thrush shouted from the topmost branch of an ash tree, the old man opened the door of the outhouse and let in the sun. Chek spread his wings and flew to meet the light. High above the town he circled once, and the old man watched as his form dwindled to a speck, and then a star that vanished into the sun.

19

Vega

Below the moor the broad sweep of the hillside was clad in a panoply of gray green oaks, somber in the gray light of early morning but tipped with gold when the spring sunshine touched the topmost twigs. At the edge of the wood stood a small, whitewashed cottage and beyond that, a narrow lane, bordered by small fields.

A collared dove flew out of the trees, perched on the telephone wires outside the house, and began to coo. Its voice had a raucous note, similar to that of wood pigeons and rock doves, but harsher, more strident, as though the bird were suffering from a severe throat infection.

At the sound a man working by the window of the cottage raised his head and sighed. For three days now he had been harassed by the shouting of the bird. It had wakened him from sleep and disturbed him at his work, and only the previous day he had discovered that the bird was one of a pair. As a painter of wildlife, he knew a little about the fecundity of the collared dove. Any time now the hen would lay two eggs. The eggs would be hatched in a fortnight, and three weeks later the young would leave the nest. This pair might have five broods before the autumn, and the thought of twelve collared doves, all croaking in chorus on the telephone wire, was more than he could bear.

Rather gloomily, he reflected that forty years ago the nearest collared doves to his cottage were on the other side of Europe, in Yugoslavia, and since then they had colonized an entire continent. All collared doves shared the same delight in perching on telephone wires and electricity cables. It was as if man had assisted in the population explosion by providing the doves with the one essential hitherto lacking in their environment, thousands of miles of perches.

It would have been a simple matter for the man to shoot the dove, but this would have been a negation of all his principles and beliefs. Besides, the death penalty seemed an unduly harsh punishment for having a hoarse voice. He went to the window and rapped loudly on the pane, waving a piece of white paper at the bird.

Startled, the dove rose vertically into the air, and as it hung suspended above the wire a dark form whisked over the hill. It swooped low over the field, flicked skyward, and struck the dove. Next moment it had vanished, bearing the luckless collared dove away, and only the vibrating wire remained to tell of the tragedy.

Shaken at having his innermost wish granted so peremptorily, the man returned to work. An hour later he flung down his paint brush in disgust, as the bereaved mate of the collared dove began her monotonous calling from the telephone wire. Snatching up his jacket, the artist stamped off into the woods. He was rapidly becoming convinced that the only solution to his problem was to call the engineers and have his telephone cut off.

Three miles away, Chek abandoned the corpse of the collared dove and soared into the sky. He had eaten the head and part of the breast of the kill and then sat brooding by the carcass, gazing skyward. For several weeks, ever since he had been released from captivity, he had been conscious of a soft, upwelling emotion within him. He was aware of restlessness, of dissatisfaction, of desires that could not be assuaged by a mere change of scenery. He hunted and killed, only to find that his appetite had left him, and he haunted the high cliffs that bordered the Severn sea, seeking he knew not what. Chek was lonely.

As the days lengthened, as the waxy yellow blossoms of the primroses glowed like pale lanterns in the shadows of the oaks and the violets breathed their soft perfume to the sun, the fever in Chek grew. He planed high above the cliffs, circling in great wheeling arcs, drifting far out to sea and then sweeping back inland, over the dark hummocks of the moors. From time to time he called, the high-pitched staccato yelping of his kind, and after each call he hung listening and scanning the skies.

Days passed, and still he did not find what he sought. His sight was so keen that he could see the bumble bees a thousand feet below, rolling and tumbling among the celandines on the cliffs. He could discern movement as far away as the coast of Wales. Eastward he could look out as far as the smoke blue haze of Sedgemoor, and south to the rocky granite tors of Dartmoor. West lay the sea, but although the skies were full of birds, not one of his tribe came in answer to his call.

The spring equinox came and passed. The moon waned, the tides which had pushed higher and higher up the beaches began to recede, and the winds that had blown strong and warm from the west softened and died. As the blackthorn bloomed, a profusion of white foam among the leafless black branches, the country folk shook their heads and spoke of a blackthorn winter.

The wind blew from the east, sere and cold, and at night frost froze the mist, so that the earth wore a silver veil in which to greet the dawn. Three frosts came in a row, and the country folk prophesied rain. The wind veered south, and by late afternoon dark clouds were rising over the moors, swirling columns of mist that towered and banked and formed great billowing shapes that were lit by the dying sun.

Above the clouds there hung a star, red gold against the violet of the sky, and as Chek watched, the star grew in magnitude, until its light took form. Then Chek flew toward the falcon, who fell from the sky to greet him, her breast bronzed and fulgent with the fire of the sun.

She was Vega, a daughter of the cold north, raised in an eyrie north of the Arctic Circle, where the sun had never set. She had drifted south, following the coasts of Norway and Denmark and crossing the wide and windy plains of Holland, where men still set their nets to trap the passage

180

hawks, as they had done since the days when the kings of Europe fought against the Turks.

Vega had escaped the trappers and their decoy doves and crossed the gray waste of the North Sea, wintering with the short-eared owls on the windswept, snowbound estuaries of the Norfolk coast. With the coming of the thaw the search for a mate had drawn her west, slowly but inexorably, along the length of the South Coast of Britain, down the long rocky toe of Cornwall, and back along the north coast of the promontory, to Chek.

Together they climbed into the turbulent air currents, forerunners of the storm, that boiled and eddied above the cliffs. They made sport of the fury of the elements and rode the wild wind against a back drop of turquoise and amber, vermilion, gray, and deep dark rose. The storm broke, and as the sun dipped below the livid surface of the sea, two stars fell to earth, to roost on the darkening cliff.

For both Vega and Chek, the night was long and arduous. Thunder rolled and hammered overhead. Wind and rain lashed against the cliffs and sent twigs and debris flying through the darkness. Lightning flashed, filling the sky with forked tails of light that set the roosting gulls sobbing and wailing like souls in torment. Stoically, the falcons endured the storm, while within them both burned the fires kindled by long days of solitary wandering and hours wasted in fruitless search.

Their courtship was brief, and on the second day their bond was sealed by a union whose moments were few, but each a lifetime long, in harmony with endless space.

From Hartland Point in the West, to Selworthy Beacon by Minehead, the coastline stretches about fifty miles, an intricate maze of cliffs and headlands, of rocky shores and inlets, wide white beaches, estuaries, and coves. In the days that followed, Vega visited them all, painstakingly exploring cliff face after cliff face in search of a site for her eyrie. Chek followed, and hunted and killed and fed his new-found mate and sat bored and disconsolate, preening his pinion feathers as Vega inspected yet another crack or cranny in the rocks. Always when she emerged, dusty and festooned with cobwebs, he would fly above her, inviting her with shrill cries to join him in soaring flight above the cliffs.

Invariably she ignored him, flying purposefully away and vanishing around a headland, leaving him to follow, grumbling but faithful, and whenever she was out of sight, filled with anxiety and fear lest he should lose her. Only in the evenings, when the skies were diffused with light, and the clifftops shone golden in the setting sun, did she relax from her house hunting, and share with him the careless joys of the spring.

Vega visited many sites, some of which had been peregrine eyries for hundreds of years past. Always she found some fault, a lighthouse, a cliff path, a farm or caravan site situated close by. Vega was truly wild, and the proximity of man unnerved her to a far greater extent than it did Chek. Once she had almost made up her mind to settle on one particular cliff, when the sight of a lone observer on the opposite headland, watching her through binoculars, sent her winging on her way. Immediately after the departure of the peregrines, the man got up and hurried back to his home, eager to inform his bird-watching friends that the falcons had returned to Baggy Point. By the time that word got around, Vega and Chek were twenty miles away, and for a week afterward several bird-watchers spent many weary hours watching a bare and windswept cliff.

There came a morning in early April when Vega settled on a ledge and began to preen. She had visited the cliff twice before, and each time she had explored the same ledge and a spacious cave formed by a leaning slab of rock. Three hundred feet below her the sea leaped at the cliff wall, the waves breaking white and surging thirty feet up the old red sandstone rock before subsiding with a roar. Above her the cliff towered two hundred feet, sheer to the green line of the turf, and above that the slope of the hill was steep and treacherous. No cliff path wound its way over the tops, no farm or other building stood near. Vega's search was at an end. Here in the solitude and the protection of an environment unchanged since the last ice age, where no man dared trespass, she would raise her young.

20

The Shadow of the Falcon

A shadow flickered fork-winged over the cliff. It passed swiftly on, over crumbling, weatherworn rock and nodding pink flowers. A rock dove died as it flew from the safety of a sea cave, and Chek bore the carcass away, back to the ledge where Vega brooded over her young.

Slowly, the peregrines were returning, to recolonize their age-old territories on the ancient cliffs and ramparts of the coast. They came from the wild places, those shrinking sanctuaries where man has yet to set his signature of doom. They may yet survive and live to share and add their token to the richness of the living world.

Their fate is our fate, for, be it good or evil, we share a common destiny. The threads of circumstance that bind us to the salmon and the whale and the birds of the air, though long, are as binding as the bonds that link the falcon to the glove on the falconer's fist, and we sever them at our peril.

Change, death, and slow dissolution is the order of life, but the resilience of life in the face of change springs from its infinite variety. Each species that is lost is a step back toward the time when the earth was without form, and void.

Yet hope remains, for just as other species have learned to modify their behavior and adapt to their changing environment, so a new breed of man is emerging, who recognizes the sanctity of life, who seeks to replenish the earth. So ospreys are returning to remote lochs in the highlands of Scotland, and their nesting sites, while kept secret, are being closely guarded night and day. In the bleak mountains of mid-Wales the kite, once so common that it scavenged the streets of London, raises its young in seclusion and solitude made possible only by the efforts of man.

Wherever possible, each known peregrine eyrie is kept under close but unobtrusive guard, as from dawn to dusk men watch and wait in all weathers, lest harm should come to their charges. For this they expect no reward other than a change in the hearts of their fellow men. The law now is absolute and forbids not only the taking of eggs or young but even imposes penalties for interference or undue disturbance. Yet legislation by itself is not enough. The future of the peregrine can only be assured through desire born within each individual, a desire which transcends materialistic gain.

The eyrie on the island of Ramsey stands empty still,

awaiting the return of its rightful owners. There are many who eagerly await this day. May their strength and numbers grow, for perhaps in saving the peregrine, they may unwittingly save themselves.